D1106701

Fastened Like Nails:

WORDS OF TRUTH.
VOLUME II.

By
F. W. Boreham

1628-1847

With introductions written
by Luke Rosamilia

LAMPLIGHTER
Publishing

Published by Lamplighter Publishing; a division of Lamplighter
Ministries, Inc. Printed at Lamplighter Bindery, Mount Morris, NY.

The Lamplighter Collection is a family collection of rare books from
the 17th, 18th and 19th centuries. Each edition is printed in an attrac-
tive hard-bound collector's format. For more information, contact us
at 1-570-585-1314, visit *www.lamplighter.net* or write:

Lamplighter Publishing
23 State Street
Mount Morris, NY 14510

Author: F. W. Boreham
Introductions: Luke Rosamilia
Executive Editor: Mark Hamby
Chief Editor: Deborah Hamby
Copy Editor: Darlene Catlett
Layout and Design: Bridgette Heap
Cover Design: Lorraine Larsen

ISBN10: 1-58474-261-5
IBSN13: 978-1-58474-261-6
Cover Material: Skiver3325, Burnish, SD513K

From *A Bunch of Everlastings* ©1920: John Bunyan,
      William Carey, Thomas Chalmers, John Newton,
      Sir Walter Scott, and John Wesley
From *A Casket of Cameos* ©1924: George Whitefield

Publisher's note: The rules of punctuation, spelling, and even sentence
structure of the 1800s were different than our present-day standards.
We have chosen to keep the original format as much as possible, edit-
ing only when deemed necessary.

Preface.

May the words of history's great men of faith found in this volume ignite new passion and zeal for our Savior, Jesus Christ. The powerful truths presented by John Bunyan, John Wesley, William Carey, and Sir Walter Scott, among others, have brought many to accept His amazing grace and fervently follow His ways.

It would be difficult to read *Fastened Like Nails* and not be changed, as we are reminded of the great things He has done for us!

Mark Hamby
Ecclesiastes 12:10

Contents.

Fastened Like Nails:

WORDS OF TRUTH.
VOLUME II.

JOHN BUNYAN'S TEXT.
(1628-1688)

Few works written in the English language have captured imaginations, convicted hearts, or encouraged spirits on as vast a scale as John Bunyan's classic allegory The Pilgrim's Progress. *While he is best known for authoring this landmark work, Bunyan was also profoundly influential as a preacher, associating himself with the nonconformist movement which opposed the rigid rules and traditions officially prescribed by the Church of England. Upon his refusal to cease preaching, Bunyan was arrested and spent twelve years in Bedford County Jail. Despite his imprisonment, Bunyan clung to Christ and would not be silenced, continuing to proclaim the grace of God through his writings. It was during this time that he wrote his autobiography,* Grace Abounding to the Chief of Sinners, *and began work on the manuscript which would eventually be published as* The Pilgrim's Progress.

*His text: "Him that cometh to Me I
will in no wise cast out" (John 6:37).*

I.

There is no doubt about John
Bunyan's text. As a lover carves
his lady's name on trees, signs it in
mistake for his own, and mutters
it in his sleep, so Bunyan inscribes
everywhere the text that wrought his
memorable deliverance. It crops up
again and again in all his writings.
The characters in his allegories, the
dream-children of his fertile fancy,
repeat it to each other as though it
were a password; he himself quotes
it whenever the shadow of an
opportunity presents itself; if it is not
the text, it is at least the burden, of
every sermon that he preaches. It sings
itself through his autobiography like
a repeating chorus, like an echoing
refrain. By its radiance he extricates
himself from every gloomy valley and

from every darksome path. Its joyous
companionship beguiles all his long
and solitary tramps. It dispels for
him the loneliness of his dreary cell.
When no other visitor is permitted
to approach the gaol, John Bunyan's
text comes rushing to his memory as
though on angel's wings. It sings to
him its song of confidence and peace
every morning; its music scatters the
gloom of every night. It is the friend
of his fireside; the companion of his
solitude; the comrade of his travels;
the light of his darkness. It illumines
his path amidst the perplexities of
life; it wipes away his tears in the day
of bitter sorrow; and it smooths his
pillow in the hour of death. When
a man habitually wears a diamond
pin, you unconsciously associate the
thought of his face with the thought
of the gem that scintillates beneath
it. In the same way, nobody can
have become in the slightest degree
familiar with John Bunyan without

habitually associating the thought of his honest and rugged personality with the thought of the text that he made so peculiarly his own.

II.

On the opening pages of *The Pilgrim's Progress* we come upon the principal character, all clothed in rags, a heavy burden upon his back, greatly distressed in mind, walking in the fields and crying, "What must I do to be saved?"

"Do you see yonder shining light?" asks Evangelist.

"I think I do," replied the wretched man.

"Keep that light in your eye and go up directly thereto; so shalt thou see a gate, at which, when thou knockest, it shall be told thee what thou shalt do!"

The man comes in due course to the gate and knocks many times, saying:

May I now enter here? Will he within
Open to sorry me, though I have been
An undeserving rebel? Then shall I
Not fail to sing his lasting praise on high.

"I am willing with all my heart,"
replies Good-Will, the keeper of the
gate, "we make no objections against
any. Notwithstanding all that they
have done before they come hither,
they are in no wise cast out!"

So Christian enters in at the gate
and sets out on pilgrimage. And
there, at the very beginning of his
new life, stands the first vague but
unmistakable suggestion of John
Bunyan's text.

"In no wise cast out!"

"In no wise cast out!"

*"Him that cometh to Me, I will in
no wise cast out!"*

There, over the portal of the
pilgrim path, stands the text that gave
John Bunyan to the world.

III.

It stands over the very portal of his pilgrim's path for the simple reason that it stands at the very beginning of his own religious experience. Let us turn from his allegory to his autobiography,

"In no wise cast out!" he exclaims, "Oh, the comfort that I found in that word!"

"In no wise cast out!"

"In no wise cast out!"

We all know the story of the wretchedness which that great word dispelled. It is one of the most moving records, one of the most pathetic plaints, in the language. Bunyan felt that he was a blot upon the face of the universe. He envied the toads in the grass by the side of the road, and the crows that cawed in the ploughed lands by which he passed. They, he thought, could never know

such misery as that which bowed
him down. "I walked," he says, in
a passage that Macaulay felt to be
specially eloquent and notable, "I
walked to a neighbouring town, and
sat down upon a settle in the street,
and fell into a very deep pause about
the most fearful state my sin had
brought me to; and, after long musing,
I lifted up my head; but methought I
saw as if the sun that shineth in the
heavens did grudge to give me light;
and as if the very stones in the street,
and tiles upon the houses, did band
themselves against me. Methought
that they all combined together to
banish me out of the world. I was
abhorred of them, and unfit to dwell
among them, because I had sinned
against the Saviour. Oh, how happy
now was every creature over me, for
they stood fast and kept their station.
But I was gone and lost!"

"Gone and lost!"

"Gone and lost!"

It was whilst he was thus lamenting
his hopeless condition that the light
broke. "This scripture," he says, "did
most sweetly visit my soul: *'and him
that cometh to Me, I will in no wise
cast out.'* O, what did I now see in
that blessed sixth of John! O, the
comfort that I had from this word!"

"In no wise cast out!"

"In no wise cast out!"

*"Him that cometh to Me, I will in
no wise cast out!"*

What was it that he saw in "that
blessed sixth of John"? What was
the comfort that he found so lavishly
stored there? The matter is worth
investigating.

IV.

In his pitiful distress, there broke
upon the soul of John Bunyan a vision
of the infinite approachability of
Jesus. That is one of the essentials of
the faith. It was for no other purpose

that the Saviour of men left the earth
and enshrined Himself in invisibility.
"Suppose," says Henry Drummond,
"suppose He had not gone away;
suppose He were here now. Suppose
He were still in the Holy Land, at
Jerusalem. Every ship that started
for the East would be crowded with
Christian pilgrims. Every train flying
through Europe would be thronged
with people going to see Jesus. Every
mail-bag would be full of letters from
those in difficulty and trial. Suppose
you are in one of those ships. The
port, when you arrive after the long
voyage, is blocked with vessels of
every flag. With much difficulty you
land, and join one of the long trains
starting for Jerusalem. Far as the eye
can reach, the caravans move over
the desert in an endless stream. As
you approach the Holy City you see
a dark, seething mass stretching for
leagues and leagues between you and
its glittering spires. You have come

to see Jesus; but you will never see Him." You are crowded out. Jesus resolved that this should never be. "It is expedient for you," He said, "that I go away." He went away in order to make Himself approachable! John Bunyan saw to his delight that it is possible for the most unworthy to go direct to the fountain of grace.

"Him that cometh to Me!"

"Him that cometh to Me!"

"Him that cometh to Me, I will in no wise cast out!"

John Bunyan's text was a revelation to him of the approachability of Jesus.

V.

In his pitiful distress there broke upon the soul of John Bunyan a vision of the infinite *catholicity* of Jesus. Therein lay for him the beauty of the text. In the darkest hours of his wretchedness he never had any doubt as to the readiness of the Saviour to welcome to His grace certain fortunate persons. Holy Master Gifford, for example, and the poor women whom he overheard discussing the things of the kingdom of God as they sat in the sun beside their doors, and the members of the little church at Bedford; concerning the salvation of these people Bunyan was as clear as clear could be. But from such felicity he was himself rigidly excluded. "About this time," he says, "the state of happiness of these poor people at Bedford was thus, in a kind of a vision, presented to me. I saw as if they were on the sunny side of some high mountain, there refreshing themselves with the pleasant beams of the sun, while I was shivering and shrinking in the cold, afflicted with frost, snow, and dark clouds. Methought also, betwixt me and them, I saw a wall that did compass about this mountain. Now through this wall my soul did greatly desire to pass; concluding that, if I could, I would there also comfort myself with the heat of their sun." But he could find no way through or round or over the wall. Then came the discovery of the text. "This scripture did most sweetly visit my soul; *'and him that cometh to me, I will in no wise cast out.'* Oh! the comfort that I had from His word, in no wise! As who should say, *'By no means,* for nothing whatever he hath done.' But Satan would greatly labour to pull this promise from me, telling me that Christ did not mean me and such as me, but sinners of another rank, that had not done as I had done. But I would answer him again. 'Satan, here is in these words no such exception; but him that cometh, him, any him; *him that cometh to Me I will in no wise cast out.'"*

"Him that cometh!"

"Any him! Any him!"

"Him that cometh I will in no wise cast out!"

Like the gate that swings open
on hearing "sesame"; like the walls
that fell at Jericho when the blast of
the trumpets arose; the wall round
Bunyan's mountain fell with a crash
before that great and golden word.
*"Him that cometh to Me I will in
no wise cast out!"* The barriers had
vanished! The way was open!

"Him that cometh!"

"Any him! Any him!"

*"Him that cometh to Me I will in
no wise cast out!"* Here was a vision
of the *catholicity* of Jesus!

VI.

In his pitiful distress there broke
upon the soul of John Bunyan a
vision of the infinite reliability of
Jesus. It was the deep, strong accent
of certainty that ultimately captivated
all his heart. Times without number,
he had come with a great "perhaps"
trembling on his lips. "Often," he

tells us, "when I had been making to the promise, I have seen as if the Lord would refuse my soul for ever, I was often as if I had run upon the pikes, and as if the Lord had thrust at me to keep me from Him, as with a flaming sword. Then would I think of Esther, who went to petition the king contrary to the law. I thought also of Benhadad's servants, who went with ropes under their heads to their enemies for mercy. The woman of Canaan, that would not be daunted, though called 'dog' by Christ; and the man that went to borrow bread at midnight, were also great encouragements to me." But each was, after all, only the encouragement of a possibility, of a probability, of a "perhaps."

Perhaps! Perhaps! Perhaps!

In contrast with all this, the text spoke out its message bravely. *"Him that cometh to Me I will in no wise cast out!"*

"In no wise! In no wise! In no wise!"

"Oh! the comfort that I had from this word: *'in no wise!'*... If ever Satan and I did strive for any word of God in all my life, it was for this good word of Christ: he at one end and I at the other. Oh! what work we made! It was for this in John, I say, that we did so tug and strive; he pulled, and I pulled; but God be praised, I overcame him; I got sweetness from it!" He passed at a bound from the Mists of the Valley to the Sunlight of the Summit. He had left the shadowland of "perhaps" for the luxurious sunshine of a glowing certainty. "With joy," he says, "I told my wife: "Oh, now *I know, I know, I know*!" That was a good night to me; I have had but few better. Christ was a precious Christ to my soul that night; I could scarce lie in my bed for joy and grace and triumph!"

Perhaps! Perhaps! Perhaps!

*In no wise! In no wise! In no wise!
I know! I know! I know!*

Thus Bunyan found in the radiance that streamed from "that blessed sixth of John," a revelation of the reliability of Jesus!

VII.

Those who have studied *Butler's Analogy of Religion* will recall the story that, in the introductory pages, Mr. Malleson tells of the illustrious author. When Bishop Butler lay upon his deathbed, Mr. Malleson says, an overwhelming sense of his own sinfulness filled him with a terrible concern. His chaplain bent over him and tried to comfort him.

"You know, sir," said the chaplain, "that Jesus is a great Saviour!"

"Yes," replied the terror-stricken bishop. "I know that He died to save. But how shall I know that He died to save *me*?"

"My Lord," answered the chaplain, "it is written that *'him that cometh to Me I will in no wise cast out'*!"

"True!" exclaimed the dying man, "I am surprised that, though I have read that scripture a thousand times over, I never felt its virtue until this moment. Now I die happy!"

And he did.

So, too, pillowing his head upon the selfsame words, did Bunyan. "His end," says Froude, "was characteristic. It was brought on by exposure when he was engaged in an act of charity. A quarrel had broken out in a family at Reading with which Bunyan had some acquaintance. A father had taken some offence at his son, and threatened to disinherit him. Bunyan undertook a journey on horseback from Bedford to Reading in the hope of reconciling them. He succeeded, but at the cost of his life. Returning by way of London, he was overtaken on the road by a storm of rain, and was drenched before he could find shelter. The chill, falling on a constitution already weakened by illness, brought on fever. In ten days he was dead. His last words were: 'Take me, for I come to Thee!'"

"I come to Thee! I come to Thee!"

"Him that cometh to Me, I will in no wise cast out!"

The words that had lit up the path of his pilgrimage illumined also the valley of the shadow of death! The words that opened to him the realms of grace opened also the gates of glory! The words that had welcomed him at the Wicket Gate welcomed him also to the Celestial City!

JOHN WESLEY'S TEXT.
(1703-1791)

When John Wesley's heart was "strangely warmed" at the time of his conversion in 1738, few would have guessed this warmth would light such a fire as to leave an eternal mark upon the Christian church in England and America! Along with his brother Charles Wesley and George Whitefield, John Wesley founded Methodism, a movement which brought widespread revival to the Church of England during the 18th century before eventually becoming a denomination of its own. The Methodists emphasized the importance of sanctification in the Christian walk, and also became deeply involved in many social issues of the time such as prison reform and the abolition movement. To this day, Wesley's influence remains a substantial force within Christ's kingdom through the denominations which he played a role in establishing.

His text: "Thou art not very far from the kingdom of God!" (Mark 12:34).

I.

John Wesley made history wholesale. "You cannot cut him out of our national life," Mr. Augustine Birrell declares. If you could, the gap would be as painful as though you had overthrown the Nelson column in Trafalgar Square or gashed Mount Everest out of the Himalaya Ranges. Lecky, who is a pastmaster in the art of analysing great movements and in tracing the psychological influences from which they sprang, says that the conversion of John Wesley formed one of the grand epochs of English history. His conversion, mark you! Lecky goes on to say that the religious revolution begun in England by the preaching of the Wesleys is of greater historic importance than all the splendid victories by land and sea won under Pitt. The momentous event to which the historian points, be it noted, is not Wesley's birth, but his re-birth. It is his conversion that counts. In order that I may scrutinise once more the record of that tremendous event in our national annals, I turn afresh to Wesley's journal. It was on May 24, 1738. Wesley was engaged in those days in a persistent and passionate quest. He had crossed the Atlantic as a missionary only to discover the waywardness and wickedness of his own evil heart.

"What have I learned?" he asks himself when he finds himself once more on English soil. "What have I learned? Why, I have learned what I least of all suspected, that I, who went to America to convert the Indians, was never myself converted to God!" One day, early in 1738, he is chatting with three of his friends when all at once they begin to speak of their faith, the faith that leads to pardon, the faith that links a man with God, the faith that brings joy and peace through believing. Wesley feels that he would give the last drop of his blood to secure for himself such an unspeakable treasure. Could such a faith be his? he asks his companions. "They replied with one mouth that this faith was the gift, the free gift of God, and that He would surely bestow it upon every soul who earnestly and perseveringly sought it." Wesley made up his mind that, this being so, it should be his. "I resolved to seek it unto the end," he says. "I continued to seek it," he writes again, "until May 24, 1738." And, on May 24, 1738, he found it! That Wednesday morning, before he went out, he opened his Bible haphazardly, and a text leapt out at him. *Thou art not very far from the kingdom of God!*" It strangely reassured him.

"The kingdom of God!"

"Far from the kingdom of God!"

"Not very far from the kingdom of God!"

How far? He was so near that, that very evening, he entered it! *"In the evening,"* he says, in the entry that has become one of the monuments of English literature, *"in the evening I went very unwillingly to a society in Aldersgate Street, where one was reading Luther's preface to the Epistle to the Romans. About a quarter before nine, while he was describing the change which God works in the heart through faith in Christ, I felt my heart strangely warmed. I felt I did trust in Christ, Christ alone, for salvation: and an assurance was given me that He had taken away my sins, even mine, and saved me from the laws of sin and death."*

Here is a sailor! He finds himself far, far from port, with no chart, no compass, no hope of ever reaching his desired haven! Later on, he shades his eyes with his hand and actually sees the bluff headlands that mark the entrance to the harbour: he is not

very far from the city of his desire!
And, later still, the bar crossed and
the channel found, he finds himself
lying at anchor in the bay.

So it was with John Wesley. When
he returned from Georgia, he was
far, very far from the kingdom of
God. When he opened his Bible that
Wednesday morning, he was not
very far from the kingdom of God.
And that same evening, at Aldersgate
Street, he passed through the gates
into the light and liberty of the
kingdom.

So far from the kingdom!
Not far from the kingdom!
The kingdom! The kingdom! The
kingdom of God!

II.

It is a beautiful thing to have been
brought near to the kingdom of God.
Many influences combined to bring
John Wesley near. To begin with, he

had a mother; one of the most amazing
mothers that even England—that land
of noble mothers—has produced.
Susanna Wesley was a marvel of
nature and a miracle of grace. To
begin with, she was the twenty-fifth
child of her father; and, to go on with,
she had nineteen children of her own!
And she found time for each of them.
In one of her letters, she tells how
deeply impressed she was on reading
the story of the evangelistic efforts of
the Danish missionaries in India. "It
came into my mind," she says, "that
I might do more than I do. I resolved
to begin with my own children. I take
such proportion of time as I can best
spare to discourse every night with
each child by itself." Later on, people
began to marvel at her remarkable
influence over her children. "There
is no mystery about the matter," she
writes again, "I just took Molly alone
with me into my own room every
Monday night, Hetty every Tuesday

night, Nancy every Wednesday night, Jacky every Thursday night, and so on, all through the week; that was all!" Yes, that was all; but see how it turned out! "I cannot remember," says John Wesley, "I cannot remember ever having kept back a doubt from my mother; she was the one heart to whom I went in absolute confidence, from my babyhood until the day of her death." Such an influence could only tend to bring him *near to the kingdom of God*.

Then there was the fire! John never forgot that terrible night. He was only six. He woke up to find the old rectory ablaze from the ground to the roof. By some extraordinary oversight, he had been forgotten when everybody else was dragged from the burning building. In the nick of time, just before the roof fell in with a crash, a neighbour, by climbing on another man's shoulders, contrived to rescue the terrified child at the window. To the last day of his life Wesley preserved a crude picture of the scene. And underneath it was written, "Is not this a brand plucked from the burning?" It affected him as a somewhat similar escape affected Clive. "Surely God intends to do some great thing by me that He has so miraculously preserved me!" exclaimed the man who afterwards added India to the British Empire. When a young fellow of eighteen, Richard Baxter was thrown by a restive horse under the wheel of a heavy waggon. Quite unaccountably, the horse instantly stopped. "My life was miraculously saved," he wrote, "and I then and there resolved that it should be spent in the service of others." Dr. Guthrie regarded as one of the potent spiritual influences of his life his marvellous deliverance from being dashed to pieces over a precipice at Arbroath. In his *Grace Abounding*, Bunyan tells how he was

affected by the circumstance that
the man who took his place at the
siege of Leicester was shot through
the head whilst on sentry-duty and
killed instantly. Such experiences
tend to bring men within sight of the
kingdom of God. Wesley never forgot
the fire.

III.

*It is a great thing to recognise
that, though near to the kingdom,
one is still outside.*

Sir James Simpson, the discoverer
of chloroform, used to say that the
greatest discovery that he ever made
was the discovery that he was a
sinner and that Jesus Christ was just
the Saviour he needed. John Wesley
could have said the same. But,
whereas Sir James Simpson was able
to point to the exact date on which
the sense of his need broke upon
him, John Wesley is not so explicit.

He tells us that it was in Georgia that he discovered that he, the would-be converter of Indians, was himself unconverted. And yet, before he left England, he wrote to a friend that his chief motive in going abroad was the salvation of his own soul. As soon as he arrived on the other side of the Atlantic, he made the acquaintance of August Spangenberg, a Moravian pastor. A conversation took place which Wesley records in his journal as having deeply impressed him.

"My brother," said the devout and simple-minded man whose counsel he had sought, "I must ask you one or two questions: Do you know Jesus Christ?"

"I know," replied Wesley, after an awkward pause, "I know that He is the Saviour of the world."

"True," answered the Moravian, "but do you know that He has saved *you*?"

"I hope He has died to save me," Wesley responded.

The Moravian was evidently dissatisfied with these vague replies, but he asked one more question.

"Do you know yourself!"

"I said that I did," Wesley tells us in his journal, "but I fear they were vain words!"

He saw others happy, fearless in the presence of death, rejoicing in a faith that seemed to transfigure their lives. What was it that was theirs and yet not his? "Are they read in philosophy?" he asks. "So was I. In ancient or modern tongues? So was I also. Are they versed in the science of divinity? I, too, have studied it many years. Can they talk fluently upon spiritual things? I could do the same. Are they plenteous in alms? Behold, I give all my goods to feed the poor! I have laboured more abundantly than they all. Are they willing to suffer for their brethren?

I have thrown up my friends, reputation, ease, country; I have put my life in my hand, wandering into strange lands; I have given my body to be devoured by the deep, parched up with heat, consumed by toil and weariness. But does all this make me acceptable to God! Does all this make me a Christian? By no means! I have sinned and come short of the glory of God. I am alienated from the life of God. I am a child of wrath. I have no hope." It is a great thing, I say, for a man who has been brought within sight of the kingdom to recognise frankly that he is, nevertheless, still outside it.

IV.

It is a fine thing for a man who feels that he is outside the kingdom to enter into it.

In his *Cheapside to Arcady*, Mr. Arthur Scammell describes the pathetic figure of an old man he often saw in a London slum. "He had crept forth from some poor house hard by, and, propped up by a crutch, was sitting on the edge of a low wall in the unclean, sunless alley, whilst, only a few yards further on, was the pleasant open park, with sunshine, trees and flowers, the river and fresh air, and, withal, a more comfortable seat: but the poor old man never even looked that way. I have often seen him since, always in the same place, and felt that I should like to ask him why he sits there in darkness, breathing foul air, when the blessed sunshine is waiting for him only ten yards off."

So near to the sunshine!
So near to the kingdom!

Unlike Mr. Scammell's old man, John Wesley made the great transition from shadow to sunshine, from squalor to song.

"Dost thou believe," asked Staupitz, the wise old monk, "dost thou believe in the forgiveness of sins?"

"I believe," replied Luther, reciting a clause from his familiar credo, "I believe in the forgiveness of sins!"

"Ah," exclaimed the elder monk, "but you must not only believe in the forgiveness of David's sins and Peter's sins, for this even the devils believe. It is God's command that we believe *our own sins* are forgiven us!"

"From that moment," says D'Aubigne, "light sprung up in the heart of the young monk at Erfurt."

"I believed," says Luther, "that *my sins, even mine*, were forgiven me!"

"I did trust in Christ, Christ alone, for salvation," says Wesley, in his historic record, "and an assurance was given me that He had taken away *my sins, even mine!*"

The analogy is suggested by the circumstance that it was Luther's commentary that was being read aloud at Aldersgate Street that night.

"My sins, even mine!" says Luther.

"My sins, even mine!" says Wesley.

Forty-five years afterwards Mr. Wesley was taken very ill at Bristol and expected to die. Calling Mr. Badford to his bedside, he observed: "I have been reflecting on my past life. I have been wandering up and down, these many years, endeavouring, in my poor way, to do a little good to my fellow-creatures; and now it is probable that there is but a step between me and death; and what have I to trust to for salvation? I can see nothing which I have done or suffered that will bear looking at. I have no other plea than this:

'I the chief of sinners am,
  But Jesus died for me.'"

Eight years later—fifty-three years after the great change at Aldersgate Street—he was actually dying. As his friends surrounded his bedside, he told them that he had no more to say. "I said at Bristol," he murmured, "that

> 'I the chief of sinners am,
> But Jesus died for me.'"

"Is that," one asked, "the present language of your heart, and do you feel now as you did then?"

"I do," replied the dying veteran.

This, then, was the burden of Wesley's tremendous ministry for more than fifty-three years. It was the confidence of his life and the comfort of his death. It was his first thought every morning and his last every night. It was the song of his soul, the breath of his nostrils, and the light of his eyes. This was the gospel that transfigured his own experience; and this was the gospel by which he changed the face of England. "John Wesley," says Mr. Birrell, "paid more turnpikes than any man who

ever bestrode a beast. Eight thousand
miles was his annual record for many
a long year, during each of which he
seldom preached less frequently than
a thousand times. No man ever lived
nearer the centre than John Wesley,
neither Clive, nor Pitt, nor Johnson.
No single figure influenced so many
minds; no single voice touched so
many hearts. No other man did such
a life's work for England." "The
eighteenth century," says President
Wilson, "cried out for deliverance
and light; and God prepared John
Wesley to show the world the might
and the blessing of His salvation."

V.

The pity of it is that John Wesley
was thirty-five when he entered the
kingdom. The zest and vigour of his
early manhood had passed. He was
late in finding mercy. Thirty-five!
Before they reached that age, men like

Murray McCheyne, Henry Martyn, and David Brainerd had finished their life-work and fallen into honoured graves. Why was Wesley's great day so long in coming? He always felt that the fault was not altogether his own. He groped in the dark for many years and nobody helped him—not even his ministers. William Law was one of those ministers, and Wesley afterwards wrote him on the subject. "How will you answer to our common Lord," he asks, "that you, sir, never led me into the light? Why did I scarcely ever hear you name *the name of Christ*? Why did you never urge me to *faith in his blood*? Is not Christ the First and the Last? If you say that you thought I had faith already, verily, you know nothing of me. I beseech you, sir, by the mercies of God, to consider whether the true reason of your never pressing this salvation upon me was not this—*that you never had it yourself!*"

Here is a letter for a man like Wesley to write to a man like Law! Many a minister has since read that letter on his knees and has prayed that he may never deserve to receive so terrible a reprimand.

GEORGE WHITEFIELD'S TEXT.
(1714-1770)

One of the most influential preachers of the 18th century, George Whitefield energetically proclaimed the gospel of Christ and the power of the new birth both in his native England and abroad in America. His persistent and outspoken witness brought about widespread revival in the American colonies, sparking a movement which later came to be known as the Great Awakening. In addition to his speaking ministry, Whitefield also established several orphanages where attention was given not only to the children's physical needs, but to their spiritual growth as well. With unwavering resolve, Whitefield focused his energy in all areas of his life toward bringing others into an experiential knowledge of the grace of God.

His text: "Verily, verily, I say unto thee, Except a man be born again, he cannot see the kingdom of God" (John 3:3).

I.

George Whitefield was the first man who treated Great Britain and America as if they both belonged to him. He passed from the one to the other as though they were a pair of rural villages, and he was the minister in charge of the parish. George Whitefield took a couple of continents under his wing; and the wing proved capacious enough for the task.

In days when the trip was a serious undertaking, he crossed the Atlantic thirteen times; but, of all his voyages, this was the worst. Day after day, ploughing her way through terrific seas, the good ship has shuddered in the grip of the gale. The sailors were at their wits' end: the sails were torn to ribbons and the tackling was all strained and broken. George Whitefield, who, wrapped in a buffalo hide, sleeps in the most protected part of the vessel, has been drenched through and through twice in one night.

The ship has been so buffeted and beaten that nearly three months have passed before the Irish coast is sighted. Rations have been reduced to famine fare. The gravest anxiety marks every countenance.

To-day, however, there is a lull in the storm. The seas have moderated and the sun is shining. In the afternoon, Mr. Whitefield assembles the passengers and crew, and conducts a service on the deck. Have a good look at him! He is twenty-five, tall, graceful, and well-proportioned; of fair complexion and bright blue eyes. There is a singular cast in one of those eyes, which, though not unsightly, has the curious effect of making each hearer feel that the preacher is looking directly at him. There is something extraordinarily commanding about him; it was said that, by raising his hand, he could reduce an unruly rabble of twenty thousand people to instant silence. His voice, strong and rich and musical, was so perfectly modulated and controlled that his audiences were charmed into rapt attention. It had phenomenal carrying power. Whilst Whitefield was preaching in the open air one day, Benjamin Franklin, who was present, made a singular computation. He walked backwards until he reached a point at which he could no longer hear every word distinctly. He marked the spot and afterwards measured the distance. As a result, he calculated that Mr. Whitefield could command an audience of thirty thousand people without straining his voice in the least.

To-day, however, instead of thirty thousand people, he has barely thirty. Standing on the hatchway, with a coil of rope at his feet, he announces his text: *"Verily, verily, I say unto thee, Except a man be born again, he cannot see the kingdom of God."* The passengers lounging about the deck, and the sailors leaning against the bulwarks, listen breathlessly as, for half an hour, an earnest and eloquent man pours out his heart in personal testimony, powerful exposition, and passionate entreaty. "Every man," he cries, "who has even the least concern for the salvation of his precious and immortal soul should never cease watching and praying and striving till he find a real, inward, saving change wrought in his heart, and thereby doth know of a truth that he has been born again."

"Verily, verily, I say unto thee, Except a man be born again, he cannot see the kingdom of God." That is George Whitefield's text in mid-Atlantic because it is George Whitefield's text on both sides of

the Atlantic. In season and out of
season, in public and in private, he
ceaselessly proclaimed that message.
He felt that he was sent into the world
to call the attention of men to that
one mandatory word. He is known
to have preached more than three
hundred times from this memorable
and striking passage. And nobody
who has read the story of his spiritual
travail will marvel for a moment at
his having done so.

II.

For it was that great text about *the
new birth* that had thrown open to
him the gates of the kingdom of God.
He was only a schoolboy when it first
dawned upon him that, between him
and that kingdom, a frightful chasm
yawned. "I got acquainted," he
says, "with such a set of debauched,
abandoned, atheistical youths that
if God, by His free grace, had not

delivered me out of their hands, I should long ago have sat in the scorner's chair. I took pleasure in their lewd conversation. My thoughts of religion became more and more like theirs. I affected to look rakish, and was in a fair way of being as infamous as the worst of them." Then came the sudden arrest, the quick realisation of his folly; and the vision of the hideous blackness of his own heart. But how to cure it? that was the problem. He resolved to change, at any rate, his *outward* bearing. "As, once, I affected to look more rakish, so now I strove to appear more grave than I really was." This, however, was cold comfort; it was like painting rotten wood: he was conscious all the time of the concealed corruption. He tried another course. He denied himself every luxury; wore ragged and even dirty clothes; ate no foods but those that were repugnant to him; fasted altogether twice a week; gave his money to the poor; and spent whole nights in prayer lying prostrate on the cold stones or the wet grass. But it was all of no avail. He felt that there was something radically wrong in the very heart of him, something that all this penance and self-degradation could not change. Then came the Angel of Deliverance; and the Angel of Deliverance bore three golden keys. One was a *man*: one was a *book*: one was a *text*.

The *man* was Charles Wesley, the minstrel of Methodism. George Whitefield and Charles Wesley were, by this time, fellow-students at Oxford. Wesley noticed the tall, grave youth, always walking alone, apparently in deep thought; and he felt strangely drawn to him. They met. Forty years afterwards Charles Wesley commemorated that meeting:

Can I the memorable day forget,
When first we by divine appointment

met?
Where undisturbed the thoughtful
    student roves,
In search of truth, through academic
    groves;
A modest pensive youth, who mused
    alone,
Industrious the beaten path to shun,
An Israelite, without disguise or art,
I saw, I loved, and clasped him to
    my heart,
A stranger as my bosom friend
    caressed,
And unawares received an
    angel-guest!

But, if Whitefield was "an angel-guest" to Charles Wesley, Charles Wesley was certainly no less to Whitefield. Whitefield often referred to him as "my never-to-be-forgotten friend." In those days Charles Wesley also was groping after the light: he could not, therefore, solve his new friend's aching problem: but he could

lend him the books that he himself
was reading, and he did.

The book that Charles Wesley
lent George Whitefield was Henry
Scougal's *The Life of God in the Soul
of Man*. He read it with amazement
and delight. It told him exactly what
he longed to know. He learned for
the first time that true religion is
a union of the soul with God: it is
Christ formed within us. "When I
read this," he says, "a ray of divine
light instantaneously darted in upon
my soul; and, from that moment,
but not till then, did I know that I
must become *a new creature*." He is
a young man of twenty-one. "After
having undergone innumerable
buffetings by day and night, God
was pleased at length," he says, "to
remove my heavy load and to enable
me, by a living faith, to lay hold on
His dear Son. And oh! with what
joy—joy unspeakable and full of
glory—was I filled when the weight

of sin left me and an abiding sense of the pardoning love of God broke in upon my disconsolate soul!" His first act in his ecstasy was to write to all his relatives. "I have found," he tells them, "that there is such a thing as *the new birth.*"

"*I must be a new creature!*"

"*There is such a thing as the new birth!*"

"*Verily, verily, I say unto thee, Except a man be born again, he cannot see the kingdom of God!*"

It was thus that the *man* introduced the *book*; and the *book* introduced the *text*; and the *text* led George Whitefield into the kingdom of God. "I know the exact place," he says. "It may perhaps be superstitious, but, whenever I go to Oxford, I cannot help running to the spot where Jesus Christ first revealed Himself to me and gave me *a new birth.*"

III.

A new creature!
The new birth!
"Except a man be born again...."
What does it mean? It means, if it means anything, that the miracle of Creation's morning may be re-enacted: a man may be made all over again. He may be changed root and branch: the very fibre and fabric of his manhood may be transfigured. You ask me to explain this *new* creation: I will do so when you have explained the *earlier* one. You ask me to explain this *second* birth: I merely remind you that the *first* birth—the physical and intellectual one—is involved in inscrutable mystery.

I cannot explain the creation of the universe; but, for all that, here is *the universe!*

I cannot explain the mystery of birth; but what does it matter? here is *the child!*

I cannot explain the truth that, darting like a flash of lightning into the soul of that Oxford student, transforms his whole life; but, explained or unexplained, here is *George Whitefield!*

"O Lord," muttered Alexander Pope one day, "make me a *better* man!"

"It would be easier," replied his spiritually enlightened page, "to make you a *new* man!"

And in that distinction lies the whole doctrine that so startled and captivated and dominated the life of George Whitefield.

IV.

With this text burned into his very soul, and inscribed indelibly upon his mind, George Whitefield mapped out the programme of his life. He set himself to a stupendous and world-wide campaign; he determined that

he would carry that one message
everywhere. He was for ever on the
march; and he was for ever and ever
proclaiming, with the most affecting
fervour and persuasion, that *except
a man be born again, he cannot see
the kingdom of God.* David Garrick
used to say that he would gladly
give a hundred guineas to be able
to pronounce the word "Oh!" as
movingly as Whitefield did. The secret
was that all Whitefield's soul was in
that yearning monosyllable. He was
hungry for the salvation of men. He
remembered his own bewilderment,
his own frantic struggle for freedom;
and he longed to shed upon others the
light that had broken so startlingly
and joyously upon him. He could
scarcely speak of anything else. In
preaching a funeral sermon soon
after Mr. Whitefield's death, the
Rev. Joseph Smith, V.D.M., said
that "there was scarcely one sermon
in which Mr. Whitefield did not

insist upon the necessity of *the new birth*. With passionate vehemency and earnest repetition he cried again and again: *Verily, verily, I say unto thee, Except a man be born again, he cannot see the kingdom of God*." He found that the hearts of men were waiting wistfully for that message.

He tells us, for example, of one of his earliest efforts. It was at Kingswood. He was refused permission to preach in the church unless he would undertake to say nothing about *the new birth*. But that was the very subject on which he was determined to speak. He therefore resorted to the open fields; and the miners, in their thousands, thronged around him. "I preached," he says, "on the Saviour's words to Nicodemus, *Ye must be born again*; and the people heard me gladly. Having no righteousness of their own to renounce, they were delighted to hear of One who came not to call the

righteous but sinners to repentance.
The first discovery of their being
affected was to see the white gutters
made by the tears which streamed
plentifully down their black cheeks
as they came fresh from the coalpit.
Hundreds and hundreds of them were
soon brought under deep convictions
which happily ended in sound and
thorough conversion. The change
was visible to all."

The news spread through the
country that a cultured and eloquent
preacher was declaring to great
multitudes on village greens, at
street corners, at fairs and fêtes, at
festivals, on bowling greens and
in open fields that men might be
remade, regenerated, *born again*.
The inhabitants of towns that he had
not yet visited sent to him, begging
him to come. When, for example, he
was approaching Bristol, multitudes
went out on foot to meet him; and the
people saluted and blessed him as he

passed along the street. The churches were so crowded that it was with difficulty that he could obtain access to the pulpit. Some hung upon the rails of the organ-loft; others climbed upon the leads of the church; at every crack and crevice ears were straining to catch the message. When he preached his last sermon in the town, and told the people that they would see his face no more, they all—high and low, young and old—burst into tears. Multitudes followed him to his rooms weeping; the next day he was employed from daylight till midnight in counselling eager inquirers; and, in the end, he left the town secretly at dead of night, in order to evade the throng that would have insisted on attending him.

V.

George Whitefield made the doctrine of *the new birth* his universal

message because he found that it met
a universal need. I catch glimpses
of him under many skies and under
strangely varied conditions; but he is
always proclaiming the same truth,
and always with the same result.

Here he is, seated with an Indian in
a canoe on one of the great American
rivers! He is visiting the various
encampments of the Delaware. He
loves to go from tribe to tribe; and
from wigwam to wigwam, telling
them, by the aid of an interpreter;
that a man of any kind and any colour
may be *born again*. For hundreds of
miles, he trudges his way through
the solitudes of the great American
forests that he may deliver to Indians
and backwoodsmen the message that
is burning in his soul.

Here he is, preaching to the black
men of Bermuda! *"Except,"* he cries,
*"except a man be born again, he
cannot see the kingdom of God."* He
tells us, "Attention sat on every face. I

believe there were few dry eyes. Even the negroes who could not get into the building, and who listened from without, wept plentifully. Surely a great work is begun here!"

Here he is in Scotland! He is visiting Cambuslang; and there is no building large enough to accommodate any considerable fraction of the crowds that throng to hear him. He therefore preaches in the glen. The grassy level by the burnside, and the steep brae which rises from it in the form of an amphitheatre, offer a noble and impressive auditorium. "He dwelt mostly on *Regeneration*," the record tells us. And the result vindicated his choice of a theme. On the last Sunday of his stay he preached to between thirty and forty thousand people, whilst over three thousand participated in the closing communion.

Here he is in the Countess of Huntingdon's drawing-room! The sumptuous apartment is thronged by princes and peers, philosophers and poets, wits and statesmen. To this select and aristocratic assembly he twice or thrice every week delivers his message. *"Ye must be born again!"* he says; and he implores his titled hearers to seek the regenerating grace that can alone bring the joy of heaven into the experiences of earth.

Here he is, bending over his desk. He is writing to Benjamin Franklin— "the man who wrenched the sceptre from tyrants and the lightning from heaven." He says, "I find that you grow more and more famous in the learned world. As you have made such progress in investigating the mysteries of electricity, I now humbly urge you to give diligent heed to the mystery of *the new birth*. It is a most important and interesting study, and, when mastered, will richly repay you for your pains."

I could change the scene indefinitely. But in every country, and under every condition, he is always expatiating on one tremendous theme:

"Verily, verily, I say unto thee, Except a man be born again, he cannot see the kingdom of God."

He cannot help it. When, at Oxford, he first discovered the necessity, and experienced the power, of *the new birth*, he could speak of nothing else. "Whenever a fellow-student entered my room," he says, "I discussed with him our Lord's words about being born again." For thirty years he preached night and day on the theme that had torn the shackles from his own soul. Towards the close of his *Life of George Whitefield*, Mr. J. P. Gladstone gives a list of the eminent preachers, poets, and philanthropists who, together with countless thousands of less famous men, were led into the kingdom and

service of Christ as a result of Mr.
Whitefield's extraordinary ministry.
He often said that he should like
to die in the pulpit, or immediately
after leaving it; and he almost had
his wish. He preached the day before
he died; and he remained true to his
own distinctive message to the last.
"I am now fifty-five years of age," he
said, in one of these final addresses,
"and I tell you that I am more than
ever convinced that the truth of the
new birth is a revelation from God
Himself, and that without it you can
never be saved by Jesus Christ."

"Why, Mr. Whitefield," inquired a
friend one day, "why do you so often
preach on *Ye must be born again*?"

"Because," replied Mr. Whitefield,
solemnly, looking full into the face of
his questioner, "because *ye must be
born again*!"

That is conclusive. It leaves
nothing more to be said!

John Newton's Text.
(1725-1807)

As a young man, John Newton found work as a sailor shuttling slaves from Africa, his own livelihood built upon the backs and blood and heartbreak of the black lives beneath his ship's deck. It wasn't until Newton first tasted of God's grace after miraculously surviving a storm at sea that his heart was turned toward the kingdom. Although he did not immediately abandon the slave trade, over the next two years God continued to draw Newton closer to Himself. In 1754, Newton gave up his life at sea following a severe stroke, shortly after which he began taking steps to prepare for becoming a member of the clergy. He was eventually ordained as an Anglican priest and served faithfully in that capacity for many years.

Later in life, Newton became a vocal supporter of the Abolitionist movement, seeking to eradicate the slave trade in England. He penned the famous hymn "Amazing Grace," an enduring anthem

*that proclaims the freedom which all
people can find in Christ.*

> *His text: "And thou shalt remember
> that thou wast a bondman in the
> land of Egypt, and the Lord thy God
> redeemed thee" (Deuteronomy 15:15).*

I.

John Newton was plagued with a
terribly treacherous memory. In
his youth it had betrayed and nearly
ruined him; how could he ever trust
it again? "You must know," said
Greatheart to Christiana's boys, "you
must know that Forgetful Green is
the most dangerous place in all these
parts." John Newton understood,
better than any man who ever lived,
exactly what Greatheart meant. Poor
John Newton nearly lost his soul on
Forgetful Green. His autobiography
is filled with the sad, sad story of his
forgettings. "I forgot," he says again
and again and again, "I forgot...!

I soon forgot...! This, too, I totally
forgot!" The words occur repeatedly.
And so it came to pass that when,
after many wild and dissolute
years, he left the sea and entered
the Christian ministry, he printed
a certain text in bold letters, and
fastened it right across the wall over
his study mantelpiece:

THOU SHALT REMEMBER
THAT THOU WAST
A BONDMAN IN THE LAND OF EGYPT,
AND THE LORD THY GOD
REDEEMED THEE.

A photograph of that mantelpiece lies
before me as I write. There, clearly
enough, hangs John Newton's text! In
sight of it he prepared every sermon.
In this respect John Newton resembled
Thomas Goodwin. "When," says that
sturdy Puritan, in a letter to his son,
"when I was threatening to become
cold in my ministry, and when I felt

Sabbath morning coming and my
heart not filled with amazement at the
grace of God, or when I was making
ready to dispense the Lord's Supper,
do you know what I used to do? I used
to take a turn up and down among
the sins of my past life, and I always
came down again with a broken and
contrite heart, ready to preach, as it
was preached in the beginning, the
forgiveness of sins." "I do not think,"
he says again, "I ever went up the
pulpit stair that I did not stop for a
moment at the foot of it and take a
turn up and down among the sins of
my past years. I do not think that I
ever planned a sermon that I did not
take a turn round my study-table and
look back at the sins of my youth and
of all my life down to the present;
and many a Sabbath morning, when
my soul had been cold and dry for
the lack of prayer during the week,
a turn up and down in my past life
before I went into the pulpit always

broke my hard heart and made me close with the gospel for my own soul before I began to preach." Like this great predecessor of his, Newton felt that, in his pulpit preparation, he must keep his black, black past ever vividly before his eyes.

"I forgot...! I soon forgot...! This, too, I totally forgot!"

"Thou shalt remember, remember, remember!"

"Thou shalt remember that thou wast a bondman in the land of Egypt, and that the Lord thy God redeemed thee!"

II.

"A bondman!"

"Thou shalt remember that thou wast a bondman!"

The words were literally true! For some time Newton was a slavetrader; but, worse still, for some time he was a slave! Newton's conversion deserves to be treasured among the priceless archives of the Christian church because of the amazing transformation it effected. It seems incredible that an Englishman could fall as low as he did. As Professor Goldwin Smith says, he was a brand plucked from the very heart of the burning! Losing his mother—the one clear guiding-star of his early life—when he was seven, he went to sea when he was eleven. "I went to Africa," he tells us, "that I might be free to sin to my heart's content." During the next few years his soul was seared by the most revolting and barbarous of all human experiences. He endured the extreme barbarities of a life before the mast; he fell into the pitiless clutches of the pressgang; as a deserter from the navy he was flogged until the blood streamed down his back; and he became involved in the unspeakable atrocities of the African slave trade. And then, going from bad to worse, he actually became a slave himself! The slave of a slave! He was sold to a negress who, glorying in her power over him, made him depend for his food on the crusts that she tossed under her table! He could sound no lower depth of abject degradation. In the after-years, he could never recall this phase of his experience without a shudder. As he says in the epitaph that he composed for himself, he was "the slave of slaves."

"A bondman!"

"A slave of slaves! A bondman of bondmen!"

"Thou shalt remember that thou wast a bondman!"

How could he ever forget?

III.

How, I say, could he ever forget? And yet he had forgotten other things scarcely less notable.

As a boy, he was thrown from a horse and nearly killed. Looking death in the face in this abrupt and untimely way, a deep impression was made. "But," he says, *"I soon forgot!"*

Some years later, he made an appointment with some companions to visit a man-of-war. They were to meet at the waterside at a certain time and row out to the battleship. But the unexpected happened. Newton was detained; his companions left without him; the boat was upset and they were drowned. "I went to the funeral," Newton says, "and was exceedingly affected. *But this, also, I soon forgot!"*

Then came a remarkable dream. Really, he was lying in his hammock in the forecastle of a ship homeward bound from Italy. But, in his fancy, he was back at Venice. It was midnight; the ship, he thought, was riding at anchor; and it was his watch

on deck. As, beneath a clear Italian
sky, he paced to and fro across the
silent vessel, a stranger suddenly
approached him. This mysterious
visitant gave him a beautiful ring.
"As long as you keep it," he said,
"you will be happy and successful;
but, if you lose it, you will know
nothing but trouble and misery." The
stranger vanished. Shortly after, a
second stranger appeared on deck.
The newcomer pointed to the ring.
"Throw it away!" he cried, "throw
it away!" Newton was horrified at
the proposal; but he listened to the
arguments of the stranger and at
length consented. Going to the side
of the ship, he flung the ring into the
sea. Instantly the land seemed ablaze
with a range of volcanoes in fierce
eruption, and he understood that all
those terrible flames had been lit for
his destruction. The second stranger
vanished; and, shortly after, the first
returned. Newton fell at his feet and

confessed everything. The stranger
entered the water and regained the
ring. "Give it me!" Newton cried,
in passionate entreaty, "give it me!"
"No," replied the stranger, "you have
shown that you are unable to keep
it! I will preserve it for you, and,
whenever you need it, will produce
it on your behalf." "This dream,"
says Newton, "made a very great
impression; but the impression soon
wore off, and, in a little time, *I totally
forgot it!*"

"*I forgot!*"

"*This, too, I soon forgot!*"

"*In a little time, I totally forgot it!*"

So treacherous a thing was
Newton's memory! Is it any wonder
that he suspected it, distrusted it,
feared it? Is it any wonder that, right
across his study wall, he wrote that
text?

"*Thou shalt remember!*"

"*Thou shalt remember that thou
wast a bondman!*"

"Thou shalt remember that thou wast a bondman, and that the Lord thy God redeemed thee!"

IV.

"Thou shalt remember that thou wast a bondman!"

"Thou shalt remember that the Lord thy God redeemed thee!"

But how? Was the work of grace in John Newton's soul a sudden or a gradual one? It is difficult to say. It is always difficult to say. The birth of the body is a very sudden and yet a very gradual affair: so also is the birth of the soul. To say that John Newton was *suddenly* converted would be to ignore those gentle and gracious influences by which two good women—his mother and his sweetheart—led him steadily heavenwards. "I was born," Newton himself tells us, "in a home of godliness, and dedicated to God in my infancy; I was my mother's only child, and almost her whole employment was the care of my education." Every day of her life she prayed with him as well as for him, and every day she sought to store his mind with those majestic and gracious words that, once memorised, can never be altogether shaken from the mind. It was the grief of her deathbed that she was leaving her boy, a little fellow of seven, at the mercy of a rough world; but she had sown the seed faithfully, and she hoped for a golden harvest.

Some years later, John Newton fell in love with Mary Catlett. She was only thirteen—the age of Shakespeare's Juliet. But his passion was no passing fancy. "His affection for her," says Professor Goldwin Smith, "was as constant as it was romantic; his father frowned on the engagement, and he became estranged from home; but through all his wanderings and sufferings he never ceased to think of her; and after seven years she became his wife." The Bishop of Durham, in a centennial sermon, declares that Newton's pure and passionate devotion to this simple and sensible young girl was "the one merciful anchor that saved him from final self-abandonment." Say that Newton's conversion was sudden, therefore, and you do a grave injustice to the memory of two women whose fragrant influence should never be forgotten.

And yet it was sudden; so sudden that Newton could tell the exact date and name the exact place! It took place on the tenth of March, 1748, on board a ship that was threatening to founder in the grip of a storm. *"That tenth of March,"* says Newton, *"is a day much to be remembered by me; and I have never suffered it to pass unnoticed since the year 1748. For on that day—March 10, 1748—the Lord came from on high and delivered me out of deep waters.*" The storm was terrific: when the ship went plunging down into the trough of the seas few on board expected her to come up again. The hold was rapidly filling with water. As Newton hurried to his place at the pumps he said to the captain, "If this will not do, the Lord have mercy upon us!" His own words startled him.

"Mercy!" he said to himself, in astonishment, "mercy! *mercy!* What mercy can there be for me? This was the first desire I had breathed for mercy for many years! About six in the evening the hold was free from water, and then came a gleam of hope. I thought I saw the hand of God displayed in our favour. I began to pray. I could not utter the prayer of faith. I could not draw near to a reconciled God and call Him Father. My prayer for mercy was like the cry of the ravens, which yet the Lord Jesus does not disdain to hear."

"In the gospel," says Newton, in concluding the story of his conversion, "in the gospel I saw at least a peradventure of hope; but on every other side I was surrounded with black, unfathomable despair." On that "peradventure of hope" Newton staked everything. On the tenth of March, 1748, he sought mercy—and found it! He was then twenty-three.

V.

Years afterwards, when he entered the Christian ministry, John Newton began making history. He made it well. His hand is on the nation still. He changed the face of England. He began with the church. In his *History of the Church of England*, Wakeman gives us a sordid and terrible picture of the church as Newton found it. The church was in the grip of the political bishop, the fox-hunting parson, and

an utterly worldly and materialistic
laity. Spiritual leadership was
unknown. John Newton and a few
kindred spirits, "the first generation
of the clergy called 'evangelical,'"
became—to use Sir James Stephen's
famous phrase—"the second founders
of the Church of England." There is
scarcely a land beneath the sun that
has been unaffected by Newton's
influence. As one of the founders of
the Church Missionary Society, he laid
his hand upon all our continents and
islands. Through the personalities of
his converts, too, he wielded a power
that is impossible to compute. Take
two, by way of illustration. Newton
was the means of the conversion of
Claudius Buchanan and Thomas
Scott. In due time Buchanan carried
the gospel to the East Indies, and
wrote a book which led Adoniram
Judson to undertake his historic
mission to Burmah. Scott became
one of the most powerful writers of

his time, and, indeed, of all time.
Has not Cardinal Newman confessed
that it was Scott's treatment of the
doctrine of the Trinity that preserved
his faith, in one of the crises of his
soul, from total shipwreck? And
what ought to be said of Newton's
influence on men like Wilberforce
and Cowper, Thornton and Venn?
One of our greatest literary critics
has affirmed that the friendship of
Newton saved the intellect of Cowper.
"If," said Prebendary H. E. Fox,
not long ago, "if Cowper had never
met Newton, the beautiful hymns in
the Olney collection, and that noble
poem, 'The Task'—nearest to Milton
in English verse—would never have
been written." Moreover, there are
Newton's own hymns. Wherever,
to this day, congregations join in
singing "How Sweet the Name of
Jesus Sounds," or "Glorious Things
of Thee are Spoken," or "One There
is Above All Others" or "Amazing

Grace, How Sweet the Sound," there
John Newton is still at his old task,
still making history!

VI.

And, all the time, the text hung
over the fireplace: *"Thou shalt
remember!"*

*"Thou shalt remember that thou
wast a bondman!"*

*"Thou shalt remember that the
Lord thy God redeemed thee!"*

From that time forth Newton's
treacherous memory troubled him
no more. He never again forgot. He
never could. He said that when, from
the hold of the sinking ship, he cried
for mercy, it seemed to him that the
Saviour looked into his very soul.

Sure, never till my latest breath,
    Can I forget that look;
It seemed to charge me with His death,
    Though not a word He spoke.

"I forgot...! I soon forgot...! This, too, I totally forgot!"

"Thou shalt remember that the Lord thy God redeemed thee!"

"Never till my latest breath can I forget that look!"

The Rev. Richard Cecil, M.A., who afterwards became his biographer, noticing that Newton was beginning to show signs of age, urged him one day to stop preaching and take life easily. "What!" he replied, "shall the old African blasphemer stop while he can speak at all?" He could not forget. And he was determined that nobody else should! In order that future generations might know that he was a bondman and had been redeemed, he wrote his own epitaph and expressly directed that this—this and no other—should be erected for him:

> JOHN NEWTON,
> Clerk,
> Once an Infidel and Libertine,
> A Servant of Slaves in Africa,
> was
> by the Mercy of our Lord and Saviour
> Jesus Christ,
> Preserved, Restored, Pardoned,
> And Appointed to Preach the Faith he
> had so long laboured to destroy.

No; that treacherous memory of his never betrayed him again! When he was an old, old man, very near the close of his pilgrimage, William Jay, of Bath, one day met him in the street. Newton complained that his powers were failing fast. "My memory," he said, "is nearly gone; but I remember two things, that I am a great sinner and that Christ is a great Saviour!"

"Thou shalt remember that thou wast a bondman in the land of Egypt, and that the Lord thy God redeemed thee!"—that was John Newton's text.

"My memory is nearly gone; but I remember two things, that I am a great sinner and that Christ is a great Saviour!"—that was John Newton's testimony.

VII.

"I forgot...! I soon forgot...! This, too, I totally forgot!"

"Thou shalt remember, remember, remember!"

Newton liked to think that the memory that had once so basely betrayed him—the memory that, in later years, he had so sternly and perfectly disciplined—would serve him still more delightfully in the life beyond. Cowper died a few years before his friend; and Newton liked to picture to himself their reunion in heaven. He wrote a poem in which he represented himself as grasping Cowper's hand and rapturously addressing him:

Oh! let thy memory wake! I told thee so;
I told thee thus would end thy heaviest woe;
I told thee that thy God would bring thee here,
And God's own hand would wipe away thy tear,
While I should claim a mission by thy side;
I told thee so—for our Emmanuel died.

"Oh! let thy memory wake!"
"I forgot...! I soon forgot...! This, too, I totally forgot!"
"Thou shalt remember that the Lord thy God redeemed thee!"
Newton felt certain that the joyous recollection of that infinite redemption would be the loftiest bliss of the life that is to be.

WILLIAM CAREY'S TEXT.
(1761-1834)

Known to-day as "the father of modern missions," as a lad William Carey might more accurately have been called "a son of modest means." As a young man, Carey worked as a humble apprentice to a shoemaker. However, even at this time Carey was diligent to develop his intellectual gifts, studying foreign languages and unwittingly preparing himself for the work which God would later call him to pursue.

Carey went on to become the pastor of his village church before eventually travelling to India as a member of the newly-founded Baptist Missionary Society. While in India, he started schools to meet both the educational and spiritual needs of the local population. Carey's pioneering work in translation and humanitarian reforms changed the face of India and galvanised the Protestant church into a new era of missionary activity, characterised by a renewed vigour and sense of urgency.

*His text: "Thine eyes shall see the king
in his beauty: they shall behold the land
that is very far off" (Isaiah 33:17).*

I.

The westering sun, slanting
through the tops of the
taller trees, is beginning to throw
long shadows across the green
and gently-undulating fields. The
brindled cattle, lying at their ease
and meditatively chewing the cud
in these quiet Northamptonshire
pastures, are disturbed by the sound
of footsteps in the lane. Some of
them rise in protest and stare fixedly
at the quaint figure that has broken
so rudely on their afternoon reverie.
But he causes them no alarm, for
they have often seen him pass this
way before. He is the village cobbler.
This very morning he tramped along
this winding thoroughfare on his way
to Northampton. He was carrying his

wallet of shoes—a fortnight's work—
to the Government contractor there.
And now he is trudging his way back
to Moulton with the roll of leather
that will keep him busy for another
week or two.

The cattle stare at him, as well they
may. The whole world would stare at
him if it had the chance to-day. For
this is William Carey, the harbinger
of a new order, the prophet of a new
age, the maker of a new world! The
cattle stare at him, but he has no eyes
for them. His thoughts are over the
seas and far away. He is a dreamer;
but he is a dreamer who means
business. Less than twenty years ago,
in a tall chestnut tree not far from
this very lane, he spied a bird's nest
that he greatly coveted. He climbed—
and fell! He climbed again—and fell
again! He climbed a third time, and,
in the third fall, broke his leg. A few
weeks later, whilst the limb was still
bandaged, his mother left him for

an hour or two, instructing him to
take the greatest care of himself in
her absence. When she returned, he
was sitting in his chair, flushed and
excited, *with the bird's nest on his
knees.*

"Hurrah, mother; I've done it at
last! Here it is, look!"

"You don't mean to tell me you've
climbed that tree again!"

"I couldn't help it, mother; I
couldn't, really! *If I begin a thing I
must go through with it!*"

On monuments erected in honour
of William Carey, on busts and plaques
and pedestals, on the titlepages of his
innumerable biographies, and under
pictures that have been painted of
him, I have often seen inscribed some
stirring sentence that fell from his
eloquent lips. But I have never seen
that one. Yet the most characteristic
word that Carey ever uttered was the
reply that he made to his mother that
day!

"If I begin a thing I must go through with it!"

If you look closely, you will see that sentence stamped upon his countenance as, with a far-away look in his eye, he passes down the lane. Let us follow him, and we shall find that he is beginning some tremendous things; and, depend upon it, he will at any cost go through with them!

II.

It is not an elaborately-furnished abode, this little home of his. For, although he is minister, schoolmaster and cobbler, the three vocations only provide him with about thirty-six pounds a year. Looking around, I can see but a few stools, his cobbler's outfit, a book or two (including a Bible, a copy of *Captain Cook's Voyages* and a Dutch Grammar) besides an odd-looking map on the wall. We must have a good look at this map, for there is history in it as well as geography. It is a map of the world, made of leather and brown paper, and it is the work of his own fingers. Look, I say, at this map, for it is a reflection of the soul of Carey. As he came up the lane, looking neither to the right hand nor to the left, he was thinking of the world. He is a jack-of-all-trades, yet he is a man of a single thought. "Perhaps," he says to himself, "perhaps God means what He says!" The world! The world! *The World!* God so loved *the world!* Go ye into all *the world!* The kingdoms of *the world* shall become the kingdoms of our God and of His Christ! It is always the world, the world, *the world*. That thought haunted the mind of Carey night and day. The map of the world hung in his room, but it only hung in his room because it already hung in his heart. He thought of it, he dreamed of it, he preached of it. And he was amazed that, when he unburdened his soul to his brother-ministers, or preached on that burning theme to his little congregation, they listened with respectful interest and close attention, yet *did nothing.* At length, on May 31, 1792, Carey preached his great sermon, the sermon that gave rise to our modern missionary movement, the sermon that made history. It was at Nottingham. *"Lengthen thy cords"*—so ran the text—*"lengthen thy cords and strengthen thy stakes, for thou shalt break forth on the right hand and on the left; and thy seed shall inherit the Gentiles and make the desolate cities to be inhabited."*

"Lengthen thy cords!" said the text.

"Strengthen thy stakes!" said the text.

"Expect great things from God!" said the preacher.

"Attempt great things for God!" said the preacher.

"If all the people had lifted up their voices and wept," says Dr. Ryland, "as the children of Israel did at Bochim, I should not have wondered at the effect; it would only have seemed proportionate to the cause; so clearly did Mr. Carey prove the criminality of our supineness in the cause of God!"

But the people did not weep! They did not even wait! They rose to leave as usual. When Carey, stepping down from the pulpit, saw the people quietly dispersing, he seized Andrew Fuller's hand and wrung it in an agony of distress. "Are we not going to *do anything*!" he demanded. "Oh, Fuller, call them back, call them back! We dare not separate *without doing anything*!" As a result of that passionate entreaty, a missionary society was formed, and William Carey offered himself as the Society's first missionary.

"*If I begin a thing I must go through with it!*" he said, as a schoolboy.

"*We dare not separate without doing something!*" he cried, as a young minister.

"*Lengthen the cords! Strengthen the stakes!*"

"*Expect great things! Attempt great things!*"

III.

I can never think of William Carey without thinking of Jane Conquest. In the little hamlet by the sea, poor Jane watched through the night beside the cot of her dying child. Then, suddenly, a light leapt in at the lattice, crimsoning every object in the room. It was a ship on fire, and no eyes but hers had seen it! Leaving her dying boy to the great Father's care, she trudged through the snow to the old church on the hill.

She crept through the narrow window
    and climbed the belfry stair,
And grasped the rope, sole cord of
    hope for the mariners in despair.
And the wild wind helped her bravely,
    and she wrought with an earnest will,
And the clamorous bell spake out right
    well to the hamlet under the hill.
And it roused the slumbering fishers,
    nor its warning task gave o'er
Till a hundred fleet and eager feet were
    hurrying to the shore;
And the lifeboat midst the breakers,
    with a brave and gallant few,
O'ercame each check and reached the
    wreck and saved the hapless crew.

Upon the sensitive soul of William
Carey there broke the startling vision
of a world in peril, and he could find
no sleep for his eyes nor slumber for
his eyelids until the whole church was
up and doing for the salvation of the
perishing millions. It has been finely

said that when, towards the close of the eighteenth century, it pleased God to awaken from her slumbers a drowsy and lethargic church, there rang out, from the belfry of the ages, a clamorous and insistent alarm; and, in that arousing hour, the hand upon the bellrope was the hand of William Carey.

"We dare not separate without doing something!"

"Lengthen the cords! Strengthen the stakes!"

"Expect great things! Attempt great things!"

"Here am I; send me, send me!"

IV.

Now the life of William Carey is both the outcome and the exemplification of a stupendous principle. That principle was never better stated than by the prophet from whose flaming lips Carey borrowed his text. *"Thine eyes,"* said Isaiah, *"Thine eyes shall see the King in His beauty: they shall behold the land that stretches very far off."* The vision *kingly* stands related to the vision *continental*; the revelation of the Lord leads to the revelation of the limitless landscape. What was it that happened one memorable day upon the road to Damascus? It was simply this: Saul of Tarsus saw the King in His beauty! And what happened as a natural and inevitable consequence? There came into his life the passion of the far horizon. All the narrowing limits of Jewish prejudice and the cramping bonds of Pharisaic superstition fell from him like the scales that seemed to drop from his eyes. The world is at his feet. Single-handed and alone, taking his life in his hand, he storms the great centres of civilisation, the capitals of proud empires, in the name of Jesus Christ. No difficulty can daunt him; no danger impede his splendid progress. He passes from sea to sea, from island to island, from continent to continent. The hunger of the earth is in his soul; there is no coast or colony to which he will not go. He feels himself a debtor to Greek and to barbarian, to bond and to free. He climbs mountains, fords rivers, crosses continents, bears stripes, endures imprisonments, suffers shipwreck, courts insult, and dares a thousand deaths out of the passion of his heart to carry the message of hope to every crevice and corner of the earth. A more thrilling story of hazard, hardship, heroism and adventure has never been written. On the road to Damascus Paul saw the King in His beauty, and he spent the remainder of his life in exploiting the limitless landscape that unrolled itself before him. The vision of the *King* opened to his eyes the vision of the *continents*. In every age these two visions have always gone side by side.

In the *fourteenth* century, the vision
of the King broke upon the soul of
John Wickliffe. Instantly, there arose
the Lollards, scouring city, town and
hamlet with the new evangel, the
representatives of the instinct of the
far horizon. The *fifteenth* century
contains two tremendous names. As
soon as the world received the vision
kingly by means of Savonarola, it
received the vision *continental* by
means of Christopher Columbus.
In the *sixteenth* century, the same
principle holds. It is, on the one
hand, the century of Martin Luther,
and, on the other, the century of
Raleigh, Drake, Hawkins, Frobisher,
Grenville and the great Elizabethan
navigators. All the oceans of the
world became a snowstorm of white
sails. The *seventeenth* century gave
us, first the Puritans, and then the
sailing of the *Mayflower.* So we
came to the *eighteenth* century. And
the *eighteenth* century is essentially

the century of John Wesley and of William Carey. At Aldersgate Street the vision of the King in His beauty dawned graciously upon the soul of John Wesley. During the fifty years that followed, that vision fell, through Wesley's instrumentality, upon the entire English people. The Methodist revival of the eighteenth century is one of the most gladsome records in the history of Europe. And then, John Wesley having impressed upon all men the vision of the *King*, William Carey arose to impress upon them the vision of the *Continents*.

"We must do something!" he cried.

"Lengthen the cords! Strengthen the stakes!"

"Expect great things! Attempt great things!"

"The King! The King! The Continents! The Continents!"

V.

Having gazed upon these things, our eyes are the better fitted to appreciate the significance of the contents of the cobbler's room. There he sits at his last, the Bible from which he drew his text spread out before him, and a home-made map of the world upon the wall! There is no element of chance about that artless record. There is a subtle and inevitable connection between the two. In the *Bible* he saw the King in His beauty: on the *map* he caught glimpses of the far horizon. To him, the two were inseparable; and, moved by the Vision of the Lord which he caught in the one, and by the Vision of the limitless landscape which he caught in the other, he left his last and made history.

VI

"Lengthen the cords! Strengthen the stakes!"

"Expect great things! Attempt great things!"

"Do something! Do something!"

It was at Nottingham that Carey preached that rousing sermon: it was in India that he practised it. With the eye of a statesman and of a strategist he saw that the best way of regaining the ground that was being lost in Europe was to achieve new conquests in Asia. History abounds in striking coincidences; but, among them all, there is none more suggestive than the fact that it was on November 11, 1793—the very day on which the French revolutionists tore the Cross from Notre Dame, smashed it on the streets, and abjured Christianity— that William Carey sailed up the Hooghly, landed at Calcutta, and claimed a new continent for Christ! And, like a statesman and a strategist, he settled down to do in India the work to which he had challenged the church at home.

"Lengthen the cords!"

"Strengthen the stakes!"

He started an indigo factory; made himself the master of a dozen languages; became Professor of Bengali, Sanskrit, and Mahratta at a salary of fifteen hundred a year; all in order to engage more and still more missionaries and to multiply the activities by which the Kingdom of Christ might be set up in India. His work of translation was a marvel in itself.

"If I begin a thing I must go through with it!" he said that day with the birds' nest resting on his lap.

"Do something! Do something!" he said in his agony as he saw the people dispersing after his sermon.

And in India he did things. He toiled terribly. But he sent the gospel broadcast through the lengths and breadths of that vast land; built up the finest college in the Indian Empire; and gave the peoples the Word of God in their own tongue.

VII.

Just before Carey died, Alexander Duff arrived in India. He was a young Highlander of four-and-twenty, tall and handsome, with flashing eye and quivering voice. Before setting out on his own life-work he went to see the man who had changed the face of the world. He reached the college on a sweltering day in July. "There he beheld a little yellow old man in a white jacket, who tottered up to the visitor, received his greetings, and with outstretched hands, solemnly blessed him." Each fell in love with the other. Carey, standing on the brink of the grave, rejoiced to see the handsome and cultured young Scotsman dedicating his life to the evangelisation and emancipation of India. Duff felt that the old man's benediction would cling to his work like a fragrance through all the great and epoch-making days ahead.

Not long after Carey lay a dying, and, to his great delight, Duff came to see him. The young Highlander told the veteran of his admiration and his love. In a whisper that was scarcely audible, the dying man begged his visitor to pray with him. After he had complied, and taken a sad farewell of the frail old man, he turned to go. On reaching the door he fancied that he heard his name. He turned and saw that Mr. Carey was beckoning him.

"Mr. Duff," said the dying man, his earnestness imparting a new vigour to his voice, "Mr. Duff, you have been speaking about Dr. Carey, Dr. Carey, Dr. Carey! When I am gone, say nothing about Dr. Carey—speak only of Dr. Carey's Saviour."

Did I say that, when our little cobbler startled the cattle in the Northamptonshire lane, he was thinking only of the world, the world, *the world?* I was wrong! He was thinking primarily of the Saviour, the Saviour, *the Saviour*—the *Saviour* of the *World!*

And yet I was right; for the two visions are one vision, the two thoughts one thought.

The King, the King, the King!

The Continents, the Continents, the Continents!

The Saviour, the Saviour, the Saviour!

The World, the World, the World!

As a lad, Carey caught the vision of *the King in His beauty*; and, as an inevitable consequence, he spent his life in the conquest of *the land that is very far off.*

Sir Walter Scott's Text.
(1771-1832)

A Scottish poet and novelist, Sir Walter Scott made significant contributions to the development of English literature during the early 19th century. One of his most famous works, Ivanhoe, brought to life a Romantic view of medieval England and was an early example of historical fiction as a literary genre. In this novel, Scott also subverted conventionally racist depictions of Jewish characters, instead featuring a female Jewish protagonist whose faith and family are shown in a positive light. Scott's writings continue to delight and inspire, a fitting testament to his commitment to excellence and industriousness.

His text: "I must work the works of him that sent me, while it is day: the night cometh, when no man can work" (John 9:4).

I.

It was a very happy bridegroom and a very happy bride that came to Lasswade Cottage early in 1798. They had been married on Christmas Eve; and, after a few days in Edinburgh, had come on to this pretty little home on the banks of the Esk. Walter Scott was twenty-six; not one of his books had been written; no thought of fame had visited him; *he* dreamed only of the happiness that must be his in the new life that he had so recently entered; whilst *she* tells him that she is sure that he will rise in his profession, become a judge, and die immensely wealthy. Scott vows that he will make his riverside home the sweetest spot beneath the stars. He takes infinite pains in laying out the gardens and the lawns. In the years that followed he never looked upon any of his novels or biographies with greater pride than that with which he surveyed the mystic arch that he built with his own hands over the gate that opened on the Edinburgh Road. In this romantic home he spent some of the sunniest years of his life; and, as Lockhart points out, it was amongst these delicious solitudes that he produced the works that laid the imperishable foundations of all his fame. As you stroll about this pretty garden, and mark the diligence with which this young husband of ours has trained all his flowers and creepers, I would have you step out on to the lawn. And here, in the centre of the lawn, is a sundial. Our happy young bridegroom ordered it before his marriage, and it has been made to his design. See how carefully he has planted the creepers around it! And, according to custom, he has had a motto engraved upon the dial, a motto of his own selection. It consists of three Greek words:

"The Night Cometh!" Scott was not morbid; he was a great human. But in the sunshine of life's morning he solemnly reminded himself that high noon is not a fixture. The brightest day wears away to evening at last. He horrified his bride-elect by arranging, before his marriage, for a place of burial. "What an idea of yours," she says in a letter written a few days before the wedding, "what an idea of yours was that to mention where you wish to have your bones laid! If you were married I should think you were tired of me. A very pretty compliment before marriage! I hope sincerely that I shall not live to see that day. If you always have those cheerful thoughts, how very pleasant and gay you must be!" Poor, distressed little bride! But she soon found that her apprehensions were unfounded. Her lover was not as gloomy as she feared. He was reminding himself that the sunshine does not last for

ever, it is true; but, just because the sunshine does not last for ever, he was vowing that he would make the most of it. *"The Night Cometh,"* he wrote upon the sundial on the lawn. *"The night cometh,"* therefore revel in the daylight whilst it lasts! *"I must work the works of Him that sent me whilst it is day; the night cometh when no man can work."*

II.

The inscription on Sir Walter Scott's sundial must have been suggested by the inscription on Dr. Johnson's watch. Scott was a great admirer of Johnson. In some respects there is a strong resemblance between them. Sir Alfred Dale, Vice-Chancellor of Liverpool University, recently referred to them as "two of the most heroic and, at the same time, most pathetic figures in the annals of our literature." Boswell's *Life of*

Johnson, and Lockhart's *Life of Scott*
are, by common consent, the two
greatest biographies in the language.
The former was a new book, and was
still the talk of the town, in the days
of Scott's courtship and marriage.
And in that noble record of a noble
life Scott had read Boswell's account
of the glimpse that he once caught
of the old doctor's watch. As Dr.
Johnson drew it from his pocket
one day, Boswell noticed that on its
face it bore a Greek inscription. The
inscription consisted of the three
Greek words, *"The Night Cometh!"*
It reminded the doctor, whenever he
consulted his watch, that the daylight
does not last for ever. *"Work whilst
it is day,"* the watch seemed to say,
*"for the night cometh when no man
can work!"*

III.

It is 1831. Scott is sixty now. It is
thirty-three years since we saw him

walking on the lawn at Lasswade Cottage with his bride. Then none of his books were written; now they are all complete. Fame and honour are most richly his. His poor bride, however, had her wish. "The burial of your bones!" she wrote, in pretty scorn, in the midst of her preparations for the wedding. "I hope sincerely that I shall not live to see that day!" She did not. She has been five years dead. The brilliant sunshine of that early day has vanished; life is wearing towards its eventide. *"The Night Cometh!"* Sir Walter is spending a day with old friends at Douglas. There is a sadness on his spirit that nothing can dispel; and once or twice, as he strides across old familiar landscapes, his companions catch the glint of tears upon his cheek. It has been agreed that there shall be no company but friends of old standing, and among these is Mr. Elliott Lockhart, whom Scott has not seen for many years. Since they last met, both men have been very ill. In the old days they followed the hounds together, and Lockhart was as handsome a specimen of a Border gentleman as ever cheered a hunting field. "When they met now," says the biographer, "each saw his own case glassed in the other, and neither of their manly hearts could well contain itself as they embraced." They part at night, Scott promising to call on his old friend in the course of his own homeward journey. "But next morning, at breakfast, came a messenger to inform us that Mr. Lockhart, on returning to his own house, fell down in a fit, and that his life was despaired of." Immediately, although he had intended to remain two days, Sir Walter drew his host aside, and besought him to lend him horses as far as Lanark, for that he must set off with the least possible delay. He would listen to no

persuasions. "No, William," he said,
"this is a sad warning. I must home
to *work while it is called day; for the
night cometh when no man can work.*
I put that text many a year ago on
my dialstone, but it often preached in
vain." It may have done. But anybody
who surveys the long row of noble
classics with which he has enriched
our literature will feel that it must
still more often have preached with
remarkable effect.

IV.

The Night!
The Night Cometh!
Was Sir Walter justified in
reminding himself, amidst the
dazzling sunshine of his wedding
bliss, that the night cometh? Was
old Dr. Johnson wise in confronting
himself with that stern truth when
ever he consulted his watch? Why
not? Is the night an ugly thing? I

recall a very familiar incident in the life of Thomas Carlyle. One lovely evening he and Leigh Hunt, the poet, strolled off together amidst scenery that was full of rugged grandeur and exquisite charm. Presently the stars shone out, and added immeasurably to the glory of the night. Both men gazed upon the heavens for some moments in silence; and then the poet, to whose soul they had been whispering of peace and happiness and love, burst into the rapturous exclamation, *"God the Beautiful!"* Immediately, Carlyle, seeing only the dread majesty of heaven, sprang to his feet and exclaimed, *"God the Terrible!"* And both were right. The Night is Beautiful as God is Beautiful! The Night is Terrible as God is Terrible! Carlyle dreaded the Night as Scott dreaded it, and as Johnson dreaded it. They all three trembled lest the Night should fall before they had finished the work which they had been appointed to do. "The only happiness that a brave man ever troubles himself much about," I find Carlyle saying, "is happiness enough to get his work done. Not 'I can't eat!' but 'I can't work!' *that* is the burden of all wise complaining men. It is, after all, the one unhappiness of a man that he cannot work; that he cannot get his destiny as a man fulfilled. Behold, the day is passing swiftly away, our life is passing over; and *the night cometh wherein no man can work!*" And who can forget those sledge-hammer sentences with which he concludes his "Everlasting Yea"? "I say now to myself, Produce! Produce! Were it but the pitifullest infinitesimal fraction of a Product, produce it, in God's name! 'Tis the utmost thou hast in thee; out with it, then! Up! up! Whatsoever thy hand findeth to do, do it with thy whole might! *Work while it is called To-day; for the Night cometh, wherein no man can work!*"

"The Night Cometh!" says Dr. Johnson, and he has the words inscribed upon the face of his watch.

"The Night Cometh!" says Sir Walter Scott, and he has the words engraved on the sundial on the lawn at Lasswade Cottage.

"The Night Cometh!" says Thomas Carlyle in the pages of his first book, a book that was written among the mosshags of Craigenputtock before the world had even heard his name. *"Work while it is called To-day; for the Night cometh, wherein no man can work."*

And these three—Johnson, Scott, and Carlyle—became three of the most prodigious workers of all history.

V.

"The Night Cometh!" It came to Dr. Johnson, the Night that he had dreaded for so long! "The

infirmities of age," says Macaulay, "were creeping fast upon him. That inevitable event of which he never thought without horror was brought near to him; and his whole life was darkened by the shadow of death." It is not pleasant reading. Let us turn the page! And what is this? "When at length the moment, dreaded through so many years, came close, the dark cloud passed away from Johnson's mind. His temper became unusually patient and gentle; he ceased to think with terror of death, and of that which lies beyond death; and he spoke much of the mercy of God and of the propitiation of Christ." His faith triumphed over all his fears; he talked with rapture of the love of God; he pointed his friends to the Cross; and he confidently resigned his soul to his Saviour. *The Night Cometh!*" he had said to himself with a shudder, over and over and over again. But when it came, that night was as tranquil as

an infant's slumber and illumined by
a million stars. The night that follows
a great day's work well done is never
a very terrible affair.

VI.

"The Night Cometh!" It came to
Sir Walter Scott, the Night of which
the sundial had spoken so effectively
and so long. We have all dwelt with
lingering fondness on that closing
scene. Here he is, at Abbotsford,
surrounded by his grandchildren and
his dogs. He is too feeble to rise, but,
at his desire, they wheel him round
the lawns in a bath-chair. He strokes
the hair of the children; pats the dogs
on the heads; and pauses to admire
his favourite roses.

"I have seen much in my time," he
whispers softly, "but nothing like my
own house—give me one turn more!"

Exhausted by his ride, and by
the tumult of emotions that it has

awakened, the dying man is put to bed. Next morning he asks to be wheeled into the library. They place his chair against the central window that he may look down on the shining waters of the Tweed. He glances round upon the shelves containing his thousands of beloved books.

"Read to me!" he says to Lockhart.

"From what book shall I read?"

"Need you ask? There is but one!"

Lockhart takes down the Bible, and opens it at the fourteenth chapter of the Gospel of John.

"Let not your heart be troubled; ye believe in God, believe also in Me. In My Father's house are many mansions; if it were not so, I would have told you. I go to prepare a place for you ..." And so on. The matchless cadences that have soothed and softened and sweetened a million deathbeds fall like a foretaste of the eternal harmonies upon the sick man's ear.

"This is a great comfort—a great comfort," he murmurs.

He lingers for a while; but the atmosphere of that conversation by the library window enfolds him to the last. The Night comes; and with the Night come weariness and restfulness and tired hands gently folded.

VII.

There is only one way of preparing for the night. We must work! That is what Jesus said. *"We must work while it is called To-day; the Night cometh when no man can work!"* A good day's work means a good night's rest. Johnson and Scott and Carlyle had learned that secret, but it was from Him that they learned it. And they became the men that they were because they took His words and engraved them on their watches and on their sundials. Yes, on their watches and on their sundials—*and on their hearts!*

Thomas Chalmers' Text.
(1780-1847)

Of all the names to grace the pages of this small volume, Thomas Chalmers' may be the least well-known to-day. Yet for the poor and unchurched people of 19th century Scotland, Chalmers was a persistent champion, worthy of the highest esteem. Chalmers used his position as a minister of the Church of Scotland to advocate for the reformation of the Scottish parish system. Chalmers campaigned for the establishment of additional churches to more adequately meet the needs of Scotland's growing population of impoverished labourers. In 1843, Chalmers played a critical role in the formation of the Free Church of Scotland following disagreements over the extent to which the official Church of Scotland was expected to be subordinate to the Scottish government.

In addition to his work as a member of the Scottish clergy, Chalmers was also a respected intellectual, holding several university positions throughout his lifetime. He authored numerous collections of essays on subjects including morality, economics, religion, and natural theology. Despite all of his achievements and political aims, however, Chalmers remained steadfastly committed to Christ first and foremost. Regarding the denomination which he helped to found, Chalmers is reported to have said, "Who cares about the Free Church compared with the Christian good of the people of Scotland? Who cares for any Church, but as an instrument of Christian good?"

His text: "Believe on the Lord Jesus Christ, and thou shalt be saved" (Acts 16:31).

I.

It was a mystery. Nobody in Kilmany could understand it. They were people of the flock and the field, men of the plough and the pasture. There were only about one hundred and fifty families scattered across the parish, and such social life as they enjoyed all circled round the kirk. They were all very fond of their young minister, and very proud of his distinguished academic attainments. Already, in his preaching, there were hints of that "sublime thunder" that afterwards rolled through the world. In his later years it was said of him that Scotland shuddered beneath his billowy eloquence as a cathedral vibrates to the deep notes of the organ. He became, as Lord Rosebery has testified, the most illustrious Scotsman since John Knox. But his farmer-folk at Kilmany could not be expected to foresee all this. They felt that their minister was no ordinary man; yet there was one thing about him that puzzled every member of the congregation. The drovers talked of it as they met each other on the long and lonely roads; the women discussed it as they waited outside the kirk whilst their husbands harnessed up the horses; the farmers themselves referred to it wonderingly when they talked things over in the stockyards and the market-place. Mr.

Chalmers was only twenty-three. He had matriculated at twelve; had become a divinity student at fifteen; and at nineteen had been licensed to preach. Now that, with much fear and trembling, he had settled at Kilmany, he made a really excellent minister. He has himself told us that, as he rode about his parish, his affections flew before him. He loved to get to the firesides of the people, and he won from old and young their unstinted admiration, their confidence and their love. But for all that, the mystery remained. Briefly stated, it was this: Why did he persist in preaching to these decent, well-meaning and law-abiding Scottish farmers in a strain that implied that they ought all to be in gaol? Why, Sabbath after Sabbath, did he thunder at them concerning the heinous wickedness of theft, of murder, and of adultery? After a hard week's work in field and stable, byre and dairy, these sturdy Scotsmen drove to the kirk at the sound of the Sabbath bell, only to find themselves rated by the minister as though they had spent the week in open shame! They filed into their family pews with their wives and their sons and their daughters, and were straightway charged with all the crimes in the calendar! Later on, the minister himself saw both the absurdity and the pity of it. It was, as he told the good people of Kilmany, part of his bitter self-reproach that, for the greater part of the time he spent among them, "I could expatiate only on the meanness of dishonesty, on the villany of falsehood, on the despicable arts of calumny, in a word, upon all those deformities of character which awaken the natural indignation of the human heart against the pests and disturbers of human society." Now and again, the brilliant and eloquent young preacher turned aside from this line of things in order to denounce the designs of Napoleon. But as the Fifeshire farmers saw no way in which the arguments of their minister were likely to come under the notice of the tyrant and turn him from his fell purpose of invading Britain, they were as much perplexed by these sermons as by the others. This kind of thing continued without a break from 1803 until 1811; and the parish stood bewildered.

II.

From 1803 until 1811! But what of the four years that followed? For he remained at Kilmany until 1815—the year of Waterloo! Let me set a second picture beside the one I have already painted! Could any contrast be greater? The people were bewildered before: they were even more bewildered now! The minister was another man: the kirk was another place! During those closing years at Kilmany, Mr. Chalmers thundered against the grosser crimes no more. He never again held forth from his pulpit against the iniquities of the Napoleonic programme. But every Sunday he had something fresh to say about the love of God, about the Cross of Christ, and about the way of salvation. Every Sunday he urged his people with tears to repent, to believe, and to enter into life everlasting. Every Sunday he set before them the beauty of the Christian life, and, by all the arts of eloquent persuasion, endeavoured to lead his people into it. "He would bend over the pulpit," writes one who heard him both before and after the change, "he would bend over the pulpit and press us to take the gift, as if he held it that moment in his hand and would not be satisfied till every one of us had got possession of it. And often, when the sermon was over, and the psalm was sung, and he rose to pronounce the blessing, he would break out afresh with some new entreaty, unwilling to let us go until he had made one more effort to persuade us to accept it." Now here are the two pictures side by side—the picture of Chalmers during his first eight years at Kilmany, and the picture of Chalmers during his last four years there! The question is: What happened in 1811 to bring about the change?

III.

That is the question; and the answer, bluntly stated, is that, in 1811, Chalmers was converted! He made a startling discovery—the most sensational discovery that any man ever made. He had occupied all the years of his ministry on the Ten Commandments; he now discovered, not only that there are more commandments than ten, but that the greatest commandments of all are not to be found among the ten! The experience of Chalmers resembles in many respects the experience of the Marquis of Lossie. Readers of George Macdonald's *Malcolm* will never forget the chapter on "The Marquis and the Schoolmaster." The dying marquis sends for the devout schoolmaster, Mr. Graham. The schoolmaster knows his man, and goes cautiously to work.

"Are you satisfied with yourself, my lord?"

"No!"

"You would like to be better?"

"Yes; but how is a poor devil to get out of this infernal scrape?"

"Keep the commandments!"

"That's it, of course; but there's no time!"

"If there were but time to draw another breath, there would be time to begin!"

"How am I to begin? Which am I to begin with?"

"There is one commandment which includes all the rest!"

"Which is that?"

"Believe on the Lord Jesus Christ and thou shalt be saved!"

When the Marquis of Lossie passed from the ten commandments to the commandment that includes all the ten, he found the peace for which he hungered, and, strangely enough, Chalmers entered into life in a precisely similar way.

IV.

"I am much taken," he says in his journal, in May, 1811, "I am much taken with Walker's observation that we are *commanded* to believe on the Son of God!"

Commanded!

The Ten Commandments!

The Commandment that includes all the Commandments!

"Believe on the Lord Jesus Christ and thou shall be saved!"

That was the Marquis of Lossie's text, and it was Chalmers'.

At about this time, he was overtaken by a serious illness. He always regarded those days of feebleness and confinement as the critical days in his spiritual history. Long afterwards, when the experience of the years had shown that the impressions then made were not transitory, he wrote to his brother giving him an account of the change that then overtook him. He describes it as a great revolution in all his methods of thought. "I am now most thoroughly of opinion," he goes on, "that on the system of 'Do this and live!' no peace can ever be attained. It is *Believe on the Lord Jesus Christ and thou shalt be saved!* When this belief enters the heart, joy and confidence enter along with it!"

"Thus," says Dr. Hanna in his great biography of Chalmers, "thus we see him stepping from the treacherous ground of 'Do and live!' to place

his feet upon the firm foundation of
*'Believe on the Lord Jesus Christ and
thou shalt be saved!'*"

Do!—The Ten Commandments—
that was his theme at Kilmany for
eight long years!

Believe!—The Commandment that
includes all the Commandments—
that was the word that transformed
his life and transfigured his ministry!

*"Believe on the Lord Jesus Christ
and thou shalt be saved!"*

V.

The result of that change we have
partly seen. But only partly. We have
seen it from the point of view of *the
pew*. We have seen the farmer-folk of
Kilmany astonished as they caught a
new note in the minister's preaching,
a new accent in the minister's voice.
But we must see the change from the
point of view of the pulpit. And, as
seen from the pulpit, the result of

the transformation was even more surprising and sensational. Chalmers alone can tell that story, and we must let him tell it in his own way. The twelve years at Kilmany—the eight *before* the change, and the four *after* it—have come to an end at last; and, at a special meeting called for the purpose, Mr. Chalmers is taking a sorrowful farewell of his first congregation. The farmers and their wives have driven in from far and near. Their minister has been called to a great city charge; they are proud of it; but they find it hard to give him up. The valedictory speeches have all been made, and now Mr. Chalmers rises to reply. After a feeling acknowledgement of the compliments paid him, he utters one of the most impressive and valuable testimonies to which any minister ever gave expression. "I cannot but record," he says, "the effect of an actual though undesigned experiment which

I prosecuted for upwards of twelve years among you. For the first eight years of that time I could expatiate only on the meanness of dishonesty, on the villany of falsehood, on the despicable arts of calumny, in a word, upon all those deformities of character which awaken the natural indignation of the human heart against the pests and disturbers of human society. But the interesting fact is, that, during the whole of that period, I never once heard of any reformation being wrought amongst my people. All the vehemence with which I urged the virtues and the proprieties of social life had not the weight of a feather on the moral habits of my parishioners. It was not until the free offer of forgiveness through the blood of Christ was urged upon the acceptance of my hearers that I ever heard of any of those subordinate reformations which I made the ultimate object of my earlier ministrations." And he closes that farewell speech with these memorable words: "You have taught me," he says, "that to preach Christ is the only effective way of preaching morality; and out of your humble cottages I have gathered a lesson which, in all its simplicity, I shall carry into a wider theatre."

Do!—The Ten Commandments—that was his theme at Kilmany for eight long years, and it had not the weight of a feather!

Believe!—The Commandment that includes all the Commandments—that was his theme for the last four years, and he beheld its gracious and renovating effects in every home in the parish!

"Believe on the Lord Jesus Christ and thou shalt be saved!"

With that great witness on his lips, Chalmers lays down his charge at Kilmany, and plunges into a larger sphere to make world-history!

VI.

"Believe on the Lord Jesus Christ and thou shalt be saved!" Chalmers greatly believed and was greatly saved. He was saved from all sin and made saintly. "If ever a halo surrounded a saint," declares Lord Rosebery, "it encompassed Chalmers!" He was saved from all littleness and made great. Mr. Gladstone used to say of him that the world can never forget "his warrior grandeur, his unbounded philanthropy, his strength of purpose, his mental integrity, his absorbed and absorbing earnestness; and, above all, his singular simplicity; he was one of nature's nobles." "A strong featured man," said Carlyle, thinking of the massive form, the leonine head and the commanding countenance of his old friend; "a strong featured man, and of very beautiful character." When I want a definition of the

salvation that comes by faith, I like
to think of Thomas Chalmers.

VII.

Yes; he greatly believed and was
greatly saved; he greatly lived and
greatly died. It is a Sunday evening.
He—now an old man of sixty-
seven—has remained at home, and
has spent a delightful evening with
his children and grandchildren. It
is one of the happiest evenings that
they have ever spent together. "We
had family worship this morning,"
the old doctor says to a minister who
happens to be present, "but you must
give us worship again this evening.
I expect to give worship in the
morning!" Immediately after prayers
he withdraws, smiling and waving his
hands to them all and wishing them,
"a general good-night!" They call
him in the morning: but there is no
response. "I expect to give worship

in the morning!" he had said; and he has gone to give it! He is sitting up in bed, half erect, his head reclining gently on the pillow; the expression of his countenance that of fixed and majestic repose. His students liked to think that their old master had been translated at the zenith of his powers: he felt no touch of senile decay.

"Believe on the Lord Jesus Christ and thou shalt be saved!" Who can fully comprehend or explain the miraculous outpouring of grace which accompanies the life of faith? But as I think of the transformation that the text effected in the experience of Chalmers; as I contemplate his valiant and unselfish life; together with his beautiful and glorious death; and as I try to conceive of the felicity into which that Sunday night he entered, I can form an idea.

The End.

BOOKS BY A.L.O.E.

THE BATTLE (Sequel to *The Giant Killer*)
DASHED TO PIECES
ESCAPE FROM THE EAGLE'S NEST
EXILES IN BABYLON *(Heroes of Faith Series)*
THE GIANT KILLER
THE GOLDEN FLEECE
THE HAUNTED ROOM
HEBREW HEROES
NED FRANKS: THE ONE-ARMED SAILOR
THE PASSAGE
THE PILGRIM'S CALL
PRIDE AND HIS PRISONERS
RESCUED FROM EGYPT *(Heroes of Faith Series)*
THE ROBBERS' CAVE
THE SHEPHERD OF BETHLEHEM *(Heroes of Faith Series)*
TRIUMPH OVER MIDIAN *(Heroes of Faith Series)*
THE WANDERER IN AFRICA

A.L.O.E. (1821-1893) was born Charlotte Maria Tucker near Barnet, Middlesex, England. She was the sixth child of her parents and was educated at home. Under the pseudonym A.L.O.E. (A Lady of England), she wrote over 140 books for children, most with an obvious moral, and devoted the proceeds to charity. In 1875, she left England for India and spent the rest of her life there, engaged in missionary work.

1-888-A-GOSPEL • 1-888-246-7735

Books by
Mrs. O.F. Walton

Mrs. O.F. Walton (1849-1939) was born Amy Catherine Deck in Kent, England. Shortly after her marriage to Octavius Frank Walton, the couple moved to Jerusalem, where Octavius ministered in a church on Mount Zion and Amy wrote *A Peep Behind the Scenes*. Her book *Christie's Old Organ* was one of the earliest books in history of both Christian and children's literature to be translated and published in Japan.

WWW.LAMPLIGHTER.NET

Books by
Christoph von Schmid

Christoph von Schmid (1768-1854) was born in Bavaria, studied theology, and became an ordained priest in 1791. In 1796 he was placed at the head of a large school, where he began writing stories for children, reading them after school hours as a reward, on condition that the children would write the stories down at home. In 1841, he published a complete edition of his scattered writings in 24 volumes. He is considered the pioneer writer of books for children, and his stories have been translated into at least 24 languages.

1-888-A-GOSPEL • 1-888-246-7735

Books by Amy Le Feuvre

The Captain's Sword
Hero Prince and the Odd One
Jill's Red Bag
The Locked Cupboard
Me and Nobbles
Probable Sons
A Puzzling Pair
The Secret Bridge
A 'Strordinary Little Maid
Teddy's Button
The Treasure of the Secret Cove
An Unexpected Offer

Amy Le Feuvre (1861-1929) was born in London, England, and grew up in a large family. She was a prolific author of children's books with a strong Christian message. Her book *Teddy's Button* was one of the most popular of all late Victorian children's stories.

WWW.LAMPLIGHTER.NET

Books of the Year

*Books of the Year are determined by
biblical insights, captivating plots, and
life-changing character lessons.*

ILLUSTRATED BOOKS

We are delighted to present to you this creative collection with beautiful illustrations for young visual learners. Reinforce character building and stimulate imagination with our Illustrated Collection. To view the complete collection, visit *www.lamplighter.net*.

Written by Mark Hamby, *Really* written by Debbie Hamby
Illustrated by Jennifer Brandon

THIS adorable adventure is bursting with colorful imagery to heighten a child's imagination and stir creativity. Learn about selfishness, pride, and vanity through the characters of Brawny, Smarty, and Beauty, and be inspired by our hero Trusty, who courageously tries to help. This will surely become a family favorite to be read over and over again!

THE THREE WEAVERS, ILLUSTRATED
Rewritten by Mark Hamby
Illustrated by Jennifer Brandon

A DELIGHTFUL allegory for fathers to read with their daughters—not just once, but over and over again. This illustrated rendition reveals how each weaver prepares his daughter to weave a mantle perfectly suited for the prince. But each father uses a different approach, and the consequences are very revealing! Enjoy many thought-provoking conversations, creating memories for years to come.

LAMPLIGHTER THEATRE

Lamplighter Theatre helps to fulfill the mission of Lamplighter by bringing redemptive hope to the world through dramatic audio. Forged through the commitment and sacrifice of a dedicated team, Lamplighter Theatre now airs on 1800 radio stations in 29 countries.

SIR MALCOLM AND THE MISSING PRINCE
2-DISC AUDIO DRAMA

Inside the castle walls a battle rages in the heart of a widowed king. His son, the young Prince Hubert, has proven himself to be an unworthy heir to the throne. But a bold intervention by the king's most trusted knight could prove to be the cure. In the remote lands of this vast kingdom, far from the walls of the palace, Hugh will learn that the requirement of kingship is servanthood. *Best for ages 6-11.*

Approximate Time: 2 hrs

The events that lead up to Betty's pivotal decision demonstrate the true meaning of humility, servanthood, and love. Inspired by a true story, Betty must come face to face with a dreaded foe. Facing myriad trials, including abandonment and the death-grip of a terrifying blizzard,

her love for her devoted servant trumps all. You will fall in love with Betty, whose loyalty is demonstrated through tremendous courage and sacrifice. *Frozen Fire* will keep you on the edge of your seat! Great for the entire family.

Approximate Time: 2 hrs.

Learn more, listen to samples, and view entire drama collection at

WWW.LAMPLIGHTER.NET

Best For...

The 'Best For' Collections are designed for those individuals who have seen this engaging collection of books and wondered which would be best for their children. We have selected an array of stories for each age group to give you just a taste of what Lamplighter books are all about.

Best For Ages 6-11

Basil; Or, Honesty and Industry
Christie's Old Organ
The Giant Killer
Helen's Temper
Jack the Conqueror
Jessica's First Prayer
Jill's Red Bag

Joseph's Shield
Little Sir Galahad
Little Threads
Probable Sons
Teddy's Button
The White Dove

Best For Ages 9-14

The Basket of Flowers
The Captive
The Golden Thread
The Hedge of Thorns
The Little Lamb
My Golden Ship
Hand on the Bridle

A Peep Behind the Scenes
Rising to the Top
The Robbers' Cave
Rosa of Linden Castle
Shipwrecked, But Not Lost
Trapped Beneath the Surface
The White Knights

Best For Ages 12-99

The Alabaster Box
Escape from the Eagle's Nest
The Haunted Room
The Hidden Hand
Ishmael

The Lamplighter
The Lost Clue
Sir Knight of the
  Splendid Way
The White Gypsy

*my*LAMPLIGHTER
BOOK & AUDIO CLUB

The *myLamplighter Book Club* allows you to follow your own personalized strategic plan as you make a wise investment for your family. We are offering you the opportunity to own the entire Lamplighter collection at your own pace, so that you are in control of your investment.

- SIMPLICITY – YOU choose which titles you would like to receive each month.
- SAVINGS – YOU decide how much money you'd like to save each month!
- CONVENIENCE – YOU maintain and update your account anytime, anywhere.

You can switch plans or temporarily put your club on hold.
You can remove titles from your queue.
You can update and maintain your account online.
Shipping is FREE! *Book Club is not offered outside the US.*
Membership is FREE!
Character Comprehension Quizzes are FREE - $199 value!

PLAN 1
PLAN 2
PLAN 3
PLAN 4

TO SIGN UP...
Log in at *www.lamplighter.net/book-audio-club*.

1-888-A-GOSPEL • 1-888-246-7735

THE
LAMPLIGHTER MISSION

Printing books of high quality with an emphasis on character development, biblical insights, artistic design, excellence, and skilled craftsmanship is an integral part of the Lamplighter Mission. Guided by our mission "to make ready a people prepared for the Lord" (Luke 1:17), Lamplighter Publishing and Bindery is strategically engaged by building Christlike character one story at a time. Through the mystery and adventure of Lamplighter stories, the framework of character development is formed and the pursuit of excellence is cultivated. The dominant theme of hope is developed by characters who persevere in adversity, being fully convinced that nothing is impossible with God.

It is the Lamplighter commitment that each book instills moral values through role models that either demonstrate exemplary behavior or suffer the consequences of making wrong choices. A riveting plot, a worthy theme, and endearing characters will motivate readers, both young and old, to adopt a similar moral code by emulating the characters that have now been etched into their awakened conscience.

The goal of Lamplighter Ministries is to cultivate a renaissance of creative excellence that inspires one to know God intimately and proclaim Him passionately. At the Lamplighter Guild, students have the opportunity to work alongside world-class actors, scriptwriters, sound designers, music composers, oil painters, theologians, culinary artists, and other master teachers.

Through these masters, Lamplighter Theatre was established, providing a platform from which Lamplighter books are adapted into classic audio dramas now aired in 29 countries. Lamplighter Ministries stands on the shoulders of those who have built a good foundation. It is our commitment to remain faithful to these high standards and inspire others to do the same and more. In the words of Solomon, "Do you see a man skillful in his work? He will stand before kings; he will not stand before obscure men" (Proverbs 22:29).

For more information about
Lamplighter Ministries,
visit www.lamplighter.net
or www.lamplighterguild.com.
To order a free catalog go to
www.lamplighter.net or call toll free
1-888-A-GOSPEL (1-888-246-7735).

LAMPLIGHTER
Publishing

BUILDING CHRISTLIKE CHARACTER ... ONE STORY AT A TIME

A DIVISION OF LAMPLIGHTER MINISTRIES INTERNATIONAL

FASTENED LIKE NAILS, VOLUME II,

FLESCH-KINKAID GRADE LEVEL: 6.3

BIBLICAL INSIGHTS: PP. 8, 11, 25, 28, 45, 49, 68, 69, 90, 94, 100, 111, 114, 128, 136..

CHARACTER TRAITS: faith, forgiveness, thankfulness

To request a catalog, please contact us:
Phone: 1-888-A-GOSPEL (1-888-246-7735)
or 1-570-585-1314
Email: *mail@lamplighter.net*
or visit our website at *www.lamplighter.net*.

ISBN 978-1-58474-261-6

9 781584 742616 >